GUIDE TO THOMAS AQUINAS

GUIDE TO
Thomas Aquinas

BY

Josef Pieper

—

TRANSLATED FROM THE GERMAN BY

RICHARD AND CLARA WINSTON

UNIVERSITY OF NOTRE DAME PRESS
Notre Dame, Indiana 46556

Original German title: *Hinführung zu Thomas von Aquin*

Kösel-Verlag, Munich

English translation © 1962 by Pantheon Books,

A Division of Random House, Inc.

Library of Congress Catalog Card Number: 86-40588

MANUFACTURED IN THE U.S.A.

Notre Dame Press edition 1987

CONTENTS

V

But for Thomas, Aristotle would no longer speak to our intellects. The problem of "unhistorical" interpretation. The medieval university: in spite of the faculty's doctrinal powers, not a part of the hierarchy; an institution for all of Christendom; tie to the city. Paris: the purest embodiment of the idea of a university.

VI

Thomas and Paris, "his natural arena." The "Mendicant Controversy"; the mendicant orders invade the university. The first years of teaching. Beginnings of the written works.

VII

Disputation as a literary form. Origins in the Platonic dialogue and the Aristotelian *Topics*. The structural form of the *articulus* in the works of Thomas. Spirit of disputation: listening to the interlocutor; respecting his argument and person; addressing oneself to him; refraining from arbitrary jargon; seeking clarity, not sensationalism. The disputation as the realm in which universality is achieved. Possible reason for the degeneration of public discussion today: the lack of proper models.

VIII

Thomas above all a teacher—in spite of multifarious special assignments. Teaching as a mode of intellectual life. Thinking from the beginner's point of view. Mastery of the pedagogue's trade. Bird's-eye view of the "major works." The *opuscula;* the commentaries; the *Quaestiones disputatae;* the two Summas. The *Summa theologica* as reflection of events.

IX

X

XI

XII

Philosophy and theology both deal with the Whole of reality—insofar as the encountered phenomena are seen by the gaze fixed upon them and insofar as the "speech of God" is heard by believers. The problem of methodologically neat delimitation is extraneous here: both philosopher and theologian must be ready to incorporate any available information on reality into their intellectual structures. *Ancilla theologiae?* Theology stands in need of the totality of natural knowledge of the world. The *Summa theologica* not a "closed system." Its fragmentary character is part of its statement. Negative theology and negative philosophy. Immunization against false claims of finality. 147

PREFACE

This book is closer to the spoken than to the written language. It is based on a series of university lectures given before collective student bodies. Its purpose and scope are precisely what the title suggests: to serve as a guide and introduction. It is intended neither as a detailed biography of Thomas nor as a systematic and comprehensive interpretation of his doctrines. Nor is it meant to be an original contribution to the historical study of medieval philosophy. Everyone acquainted with the field will see at once to what degree my account is based, far beyond specific quotation, on the works of Marie-Dominique Chenu, Étienne Gilson, Fernand van Steenberghen, and others.

The purpose of these lectures is to sketch, against the background of his times and his life, a portrait of Thomas Aquinas as he truly concerns philosophical-minded persons today, not merely as a historical personage but as a thinker who has something to say to our own era. I earnestly hope that the speculative attitude which was Thomas' most salient trait as Christianity's "universal teacher" will emerge clearly and sharply from my exposition. It is to this end alone, I repeat, that I present the following chapters, and it is this aspect for which I accept full responsibility.

J. P.

GUIDE TO THOMAS AQUINAS

I

So bound up is the life of St. Thomas Aquinas with the thirteenth century that the year in which the century reached its mid-point, 1250, was likewise the mid-point of Thomas' life, though he was only twenty-five years old at the time and still sitting at the feet of Albertus Magnus as a student in the Monastery of the Holy Cross in Cologne. The thirteenth century has been called the specifically "Occidental" century. The significance of this epithet has not always been completely clarified, but in a certain sense I too accept the term. I would even assert that the special quality of "Occidentality" was ultimately forged in that very century, and by Thomas Aquinas himself. It depends, however, on what we understand by "Occidentality." We shall have more to say on this matter.

There exists the romantic notion that the thirteenth century was an era of harmonious balance, of stable order, and of the free flowering of Christianity. Especially in the realm of thought, this was not so. The Louvain historian Fernand van Steenberghen speaks of the thirteenth century as a time of "crisis of Christian intelligence";[1] and Gilson comments: "Anybody could see that a crisis was brewing."[2]

What, in concrete terms, was the situation? First of all we must point out that Christianity, already besieged by Islam for centuries, threatened by the mounted hordes of Asiatics (1241 is the year of the battle with the Mongols at Liegnitz)—that this Christianity of the thirteenth century had been drastically reminded of how small a body it was within a vast non-Christian world. It was learning its own limits in the most forceful way, and those limits were not only territorial. Around 1253 or 1254 the court of the Great Khan in Karakorum, in the heart of Asia, was the scene of a disputation of two French mendicant friars with Mohammedans and Buddhists. Whether we can conclude that these friars represented a "universal mission sent forth out of disillusionment with the old Christianity,"[3] is more than questionable. But be this as it may, Christianity saw itself subjected to a grave challenge, and not only from the areas beyond its territorial limits.

For a long time the Arab world, which had thrust itself into old Europe, had been impressing Christians not only with its military and political might but also with its philosophy and science. Through translations from the Arabic into Latin, Arab philosophy and Arab science had become firmly established in the heart of Christendom—at the University of Paris, for example. Looking into the matter more closely, of course, we are struck by the fact that Arab philosophy and science were not Islamic by origin and character. Rather, classical *ratio,* epitomized by Aristotle, had by such strangely involved routes come to penetrate the intellectual world of Christian Europe. But in the beginning, at any rate, it was felt as something alien, new, dangerous, "pagan."

During this same period, thirteenth-century Christendom was being shaken politically from top to bottom. Internal upheavals of every sort were brewing. Christendom was entering upon the age "in which it would cease to be a theocratic unity,"[4] and would, in fact, never be so again. In 1214 a national king (as such) for the first time won a victory over the Emperor (as such) at the Battle of Bouvines. During this same period the first religious wars within Christendom flared up, to be waged with inconceivable cruelty on both sides. Such was the effect of these conflicts that all of southern France and northern Italy seemed for

4

decades to be lost once and for all to the corpus of Christendom. Old monasticism, which was invoked as a spiritual counterforce, seems (as an institution, that is to say, seen as a whole) to have become impotent, in spite of all heroic efforts to reform it (Cluny, Cîteaux, etc.). And as far as the bishops were concerned—and here, too, of course, we are making a sweeping statement—an eminent Dominican prior of Louvain, who incidentally may have been a fellow pupil of St. Thomas under Albertus Magnus in Cologne, wrote the following significant homily: In 1248 it happened at Paris that a cleric was to preach before a synod of bishops; and while he was considering what he should say, the devil appeared to him. "Tell them this alone," the devil said. "The princes of infernal darkness offer the princes of the Church their greetings. We thank them heartily for leading their charges to us and commend the fact that due to their negligence almost the entire world is succumbing to darkness."[5]

But of course it could not be that Christianity should passively succumb to these developments. Thirteenth-century Christianity rose in its own defense, and in a most energetic fashion. Not only were great cathedrals built in that century; it saw also the founding of the first universities. The universities undertook, among other things, the task of assimilating classical ideas and philosophy, and to a large extent accomplished this task.

There was also the whole matter of the "mendicant orders," which represented one of the most creative responses of Christianity. These new associations quite unexpectedly allied themselves with the institution of the university. The most important university teachers of the century, in Paris as well as in Oxford, were all monks of the mendicant orders. All in all, nothing seemed to be "finished"; everything had entered a state of flux. Albertus

Magnus voiced this bold sense of futurity in the words: *Scientiae demonstrativae non omnes factae sunt, sed plures restant adhuc inveniendae;* most of what exists in the realm of knowledge remains still to be discovered.[6]

The mendicant orders took the lead in moving out into the world beyond the frontiers of Christianity. Shortly after the middle of the century, while Thomas was writing his *Summa Against the Pagans,* addressed to the *mahumetistae et pagani,*[7] the Dominicans were founding the first Christian schools for teaching the Arabic language. I have already spoken of the disputation between the mendicant friars and the sages of Eastern faiths in Karakorum. Toward the end of the century a Franciscan translated the New Testament and the Psalms into Mongolian and presented this translation to the Great Khan. He was the same Neapolitan, John of Monte Corvino, who built a church alongside the Imperial Palace in Peking and who became the first Archbishop of Peking.

This mere listing of a few events, facts, and elements should make it clear that the era was anything but a harmonious one. There is little reason for wishing for a return to those times—aside from the fact that such wishes are in themselves foolish.

Nevertheless, it may be said that in terms of the history of thought this thirteenth century, for all its polyphonic character, did attain something like harmony and "classical fullness." At least this was so for a period of three or four decades. Gilson speaks of a kind of "serenity."[8] And although that moment in time is of course gone and cannot ever again be summoned back, it appears to have left its traces upon the memory of Western Christianity, so that it is recalled as something paradigmatic and exemplary, a kind of ideal spirit of an age which men long to see realized once more, although under changed conditions and therefore, of course, in some altogether new cast.

Now as it happens, the work of Thomas Aquinas falls into that brief historical moment. Perhaps it may be said that his work embodies that moment. Such, at any rate, is the sense in which St. Thomas' achievement has been understood in the Christian world for almost seven hundred years; such are the terms in which it has repeatedly been evaluated. Not by all, to be sure (Luther called Thomas "the greatest chatterbox" among the scholastic theologians[9]); but the voices of approbation and reverence have always predominated. And even aside from his written work, his personal destiny and the events of his life unite virtually all the elements of that highly contradictory century in a kind of "existential" synthesis. We shall now speak of these matters at greater length, and in detail.

First of all, a few remarks regarding books.

The best introduction to the spirit of St. Thomas is, to my mind, the small book by G. K. Chesterton, *St. Thomas Aquinas.*[10] This is not a scholarly work in the proper sense of the word; it might be called journalistic—for which reason I am somewhat chary about recommending it. Maisie Ward, co-owner of the British-American publishing firm which publishes the book, writes in her biography of Chesterton[11] that at the time her house published it, she was seized by a slight anxiety. However, she goes on to say, Étienne Gilson read it and commented: "Chesterton makes one despair. I have been studying St. Thomas all my life and I could never have written such a book." Still troubled by the ambiguity of this comment, Maisie Ward asked Gilson once more for his verdict on the Chesterton book. This time he expressed himself in unmistakable terms: "I consider it as being, without possible comparison, the best book ever written on St. Thomas. . . . Everybody will no doubt admit that it is a 'clever' book, but the few readers who have spent twenty or thirty years in studying St. Thomas Aquinas, and who, perhaps, have themselves published two or three volumes on the subject, cannot fail to perceive that the so-called 'wit' of Chesterton has put their scholarship to shame. . . . He has said all that which they were more or less clumsily attempting to express in academic formulas."

Thus Gilson. I think this praise somewhat exaggerated; but at any rate I need feel no great embarrassment about recommending an "unscholarly" book.

It would not do to rely on Chesterton alone, even for an introduction. I therefore recommend, for its more professional approach, Martin Grabmann's *Thomas von Aquin. Persönlichkeit und Gedankenwelt*, which has appeared in numerous editions since 1912.[12] Grabmann (died 1949 in Munich) is known and esteemed throughout the world as the master of scholastic research; his book has that very special merit which is achieved only when a scholar who knows the material from the original sources down to the last details, and who for the most part has himself uncovered these sources, writes a summary for the nonspecialist. I point this out because Grabmann conceals his deep scholarship behind an utterly plain presentation.

A more modern study is the splendid, thorough, and brilliantly written *Introduction à l'étude de St. Thomas d'Aquin* by Marie-Dominique Chenu.[13] Chenu divides his book into two parts, the first dealing with "the work," the second with "the works." I think it may be said that at the present moment no better historical and systematic introduction to Thomas exists.

Finally I should like to mention the more comprehensive and ambitious exposition of the philosophy of St. Thomas, by Étienne Gilson: *Le Thomisme, Introduction à la philosophie de St. Thomas*. A revised edition of this work has recently been published in English under the title, *The Christian Philosophy of St. Thomas Aquinas*.[14]

The books by Chenu and Gilson have, by the way, one feature in common which may at first seem incidental. The authors of both are French (Chenu is a Dominican; Gilson is a layman, originally a professor at the Collège de France), but both have taught for many years in the New World, that is to say, in Canada. That both books were produced in a very special atmosphere of that young continent seems to me more than accidental. As I read these works, I felt throughout the breath of the fresh winds of North America—by which I mean something rather precise: a certain objectivity and earnestness, the determination on the part of the writers to go beyond mere scholarliness and to ask and answer the question of the truth of things.

Let us begin with a quick biographical survey. Thomas was born around 1225 in the castle of Roccasecca near Aquino, a small town between Rome and Naples. Was he therefore a "Latin," a south Italian? Yes and no. This ambiguity is in itself important. First of all, the "yes"—Thomas *was* an Italian. We know that he later preached in his native tongue, the language of the people of Naples. And one of his brothers, Rinaldo, made a name for himself as a lyric poet,[15] his best-known works being certain love poems in the vulgar tongue which at that time—two generations before Dante's *Divina Commedia*—was becoming a national language. While St. Thomas' *articuli* are of course in Latin, their inner dynamics must be thought of as reflecting south Italian speech—that is to say, they are rapid and energetic in manner and tempo.

However, we must keep in mind that Thomas was of Germanic blood on both his father's and his mother's side. His mother's family was Norman, his father's either Lombard or likewise Norman. And the social environment from which Thomas sprang and in which he grew up was given its character by the Swabian emperors, the Ho-

9

henstaufen; his father and his brothers were members of the court nobility of Frederick II of Hohenstaufen. Taken all together, this means that Thomas did not spring from the soil of the classical Roman Empire; he stemmed from the new tribes which had overwhelmed and taken possession of the *Imperium Romanum,* first as barbarian invaders, then as "occupiers," and finally as docile pupils and the historical heirs of Rome. The times of Boethius, who had endeavored to pass on the heritage of Greco-Roman classicism to the new historical powers by translation and commentary, were long since past. The pupils had come of age.

Thomas was the youngest of the family. At the age of five he was sent to school at the nearby Abbey of Monte Cassino. Barely ten years later, as we may read in many a biographical account, he "moved" to Naples. On closer examination we discover that it was not a simple change of residence, but rather a flight. After all, it would not be quite accurate to say of scholars who had left Nazi Germany as exiles that they simply "went" to America. And young Thomas' move was likewise influenced by political developments, that is to say, by the struggle between Emperor and Pope. Monte Cassino was not merely a Benedictine abbey; it was also a citadel on the border between the imperial and the papal territories. Moreover the abbey, which had been founded by St. Benedict in 529 (the year of the dissolution of the Platonic Academy in Athens), had been destroyed twice—once by the Lombards and once by the Saracens. It had at one time lain in ruins for more than a hundred years.

I have said that the life of St. Thomas contains almost all the components of the century. A number of these components lie within this mere fact of his "flight from Monte Cassino to Naples." First, there was the struggle between

Emperor and Pope, which shook Christendom to its foundations and was to force it into a new shape. Second, there was the taking leave of the feudally constituted Benedictine abbey with its early medieval character, which was no longer representative of the age now dawning and could not operate effectually in that age. Third, there was not only the negative step of withdrawing from the solitude of old monasticism, but the entrance into a city. The entrance also into a university, the first state university of the Western world, founded only a short while before by Frederick II. Fourth, there was the confrontation with Aristotle which was unavoidable precisely at this consciously secular university, and which could not have taken place in so intensive a form at any other university. Fifth, there was the encounter with the tremendously dynamic voluntary poverty movement, with the first generation of the mendicant orders—an encounter which, again, was possible and to be expected only in a city. Later we shall discuss each of these points in detail, but especially the last three (university, Aristotle, mendicant order movement).

Thomas was about nineteen when he joined one of the two mendicant orders, the Order of Preachers founded by the Spaniard Dominic. Apparently he took this step on the basis of a sudden decision which he probably did not tell his family, but which he held to with unyielding resolution. In a polemical article in defense of the monastic estate, Thomas raises a point which may have autobiographical significance. He poses the question of whether such a decision should not have to be long considered and discussed—and answers with unusual sharpness that blood relations should first and foremost be excluded from such deliberations, since in this respect they are foes rather than friends.[16] In his own case the move was not undertaken without considerable conflict. When the Neapolitan brethren of the order endeavored to get their novice as quickly as possible out of reach of his family's and the Hohenstaufen Emperor's power (for the mendicant orders were constantly under suspicion of working on the Pope's side against the Emperor) by dispatching Thomas at once to Paris, his own brothers captured him—probably with imperial assistance—and held him for a long time in one of his father's castles. His imprisonment may have lasted a full year. In any case, he profited by the time: as Grabmann has discovered,[17] he transcribed a copy or an extract from one of Aristotle's writings on logic. Finally he was released, and continued on his way to Paris.

Thomas arrived at *the* university of the Western world first as a student; later he was to become one of that university's greatest teachers. In 1245, the very year of his arrival in Paris, Albertus Magnus had begun teaching there. Had all Europe been canvassed, no more important and more up-to-date teacher for Thomas could have been found. The two proceeded together to Cologne, where Albertus was to set up an academy of the Dominican Order. During this period of apprenticeship under Albert—incidentally, the foundation stone of Cologne Cathedral was laid at this time—Thomas became acquainted with a wholly new strain in Western philosophy: Neo-Platonism. He was led to it by his teacher. During those very years in Cologne, Albertus Magnus had plunged into the study of Dionysius Areopagita, the Neo-Platonic mystic who, by masquerading as that disciple of Paul mentioned in the Acts of the Apostles, preserved the Platonic heritage for a Christian West fascinated by Aristotle.

At the age of twenty-seven Thomas was recalled to Paris. He was employed there first at the Dominican academy in the Monastery of St. Jacques. Later he became professor of theology at the university—in spite of considerable opposition directed not so much against himself as an individual as against the ever mounting influence of the mendicant orders at the university. Thomas was drastically affected by these bickerings. The Pope himself had to intervene to cause the university to lift the boycott against Thomas. Under papal pressure the ban was finally lifted—on the same day for Thomas and for Bonaventura; the Pope's letter mentions both by name.

It is astonishing to note that in St. Thomas' first works, written during this period, the smooth flow of not a single sentence appears to have been ruffled by all these troubles. Readers of these *opuscula*, such as *De ente et essentia*, will find it hard to believe that they were not written in the undisturbed peace of a monastic cell. That, too, was a new element which Thomas embodied: cloistral seclusion became *inner* seclusion. Times were changing, and from now on it would be necessary to construct a cell for contemplation within the self to be carried about through the hurly-burly of the *vita activa* of teaching and of intellectual disputation.

Thomas experienced this hurly-burly in good measure. It is true that he gave up his teaching chair at the University of Paris as early as 1259—after three years, that is—embarking instead upon a life of wandering that lasted until his death and never permitted him to remain longer than two or three years in the same place and in the same position. One burden, however, he carried about with him all his life: the task of presenting, whether by teaching or writing, the whole of the Christian view of the universe.

First of all he was sent to Italy by the Dominican Order, on commissions principally connected with the organization of studies. Then Pope Urban IV called him for three years to his court in Orvieto where—even though the official prohibitions upon Aristotle were still in force—a Flemish Dominican who had learned the language of

Aristotle during a stay in Greece was engaged on no other task than translating the works of this same banned philosopher. Thomas himself had urged his brother Dominican William of Moerbecke to undertake this work. The Pope, however, needed Thomas' aid in an enterprise of literally universal significance. It seemed possible that a union might be brought about between the Eastern and Western branches of Christianity. Thomas was asked to lay down the theologic basis for this union.

Three years later came a new assignment, as head of the Dominican academy at Santa Sabina in Rome. Thomas stayed at this post for two years. Only ten years of life remained to him, and as yet not one of the twelve commentaries on the writings of Aristotle had been written, nor a line of the *Summa theologica.* During these two years in Rome he set to work on both. Then a new Pope, Clement IV, called him back to the court at Viterbo. This Pope was not without guilt in the death of the last of the Hohenstaufens, the boy Conradin, who met his end on the scaffold at Naples during these years. At this time Thomas was writing, among other things, his book *On the Governance of Princes,* which contains the magnificent chapter on the reward to be expected by righteous kings.[18]

In 1269, after barely two years, came the unexpected and highly unusual command from the superiors of his order to return to the University of Paris. The battle against the mendicants had meanwhile considerably intensified and taken a more radical turn. It no longer centered around capturing teaching chairs, but around the teachings themselves. Nor was this the only thing at stake. The real issue was the confrontation with two fundamental philosophical and theological views. This had a direct bearing on the position taken by St. Thomas himself, the position which concerned him deeply and which he had single-handedly been trying to formulate, clarify, and defend. At this point we cannot go into detail. We can only say that what was at stake was the special character of "Occidentality." What was more, it was threatened simultaneously by those who were anxious to hold fast to traditional Christian concepts *and also* by those who perverted Thomas' bold new concept by exaggeration.

Oddly enough, Thomas stood completely alone in this situation. A most astonishing fact comes to light: this man who was a teacher by birth, by inclination, and by grace had no disciple of real importance. Even immediately after his death there was no one who could have preserved and defended the master's heritage with a persuasiveness even remotely equal to his own. Thomas stood alone—and he threw himself into his task with fantastic vehemence. What he wrote during those last years in Paris—once more, only three years—seems almost beyond belief: commentaries on virtually all the works of Aristotle; a commentary on the Book of Job, on the Gospel of John, on the Epistles of Paul; the great *Quaestiones disputatae* on evil, on the virtues; the comprehensive Second Part of the *Summa theologica*. At the same time Thomas by no means absented himself from the great debate which was raging. On the contrary, all his works were actual contributions to it—even if we disregard the distinctly polemical writings. The debate grew ever more heated, and in 1272 the superiors of the order suddenly recalled Thomas from Paris. We may suppose that they hoped thereby to temper the intellectual struggle. At any rate, Thomas' successor to the chair inclined more toward the traditional, conservative views.

Assigned to found an academy within the order, Thomas returned to Naples, the scene of his first decisions. Here, after about a year, another papal assignment reached him, this time to participate in the General Council which was to begin its sessions in Lyons in the spring of 1274. On the way there he fell ill and soon afterward died, on March 7, 1274, having not yet reached the age of fifty.

Several months before he set out on the journey to Lyons, Thomas had already stopped writing, although his *opus magnum,* the *Summa theologica,* was not yet finished. Pupils and friends urged him to continue, but Thomas refused to write or to dictate another line. And there the work stood. "Everything I have written seems to me straw"—this was his reply to the urgings of Reginald of Piperno, his friend, secretary, and traveling companion of many years. Later, to be sure, he amplified this statement: "Everything . . . seems to me straw—compared with the vision I have had." These words point to something which falls outside the scope of these lectures, and which nevertheless cannot be passed over in silence: the fact that Thomas was not only a philosophical and theological thinker, not only a university professor, but also a mystic visionary, a saint.

In the following pages we shall review the course of Thomas' life again, at a more deliberate pace, in order to see more clearly how the work of St. Thomas sprang from the challenges of the times and his responses.

II

We must add to this first rapid and necessarily brief survey of Thomas' life a few comments on some facts which, though they cannot properly be regarded as strictly biographical, are yet part and parcel of the story of the man Thomas Aquinas.

The first of these facts is Thomas' *canonization*. I am sometimes surprised at the wild notions held by cultivated people of the meaning of this procedure—as, for example, the grotesque idea that canonization is a kind of posthumous "promotion." Naturally, the act of canonization in no way alters or affects the person so celebrated; nothing whatsoever comes into being that was not so before. Of course not! Rather, the act is an announcement—based upon a solemn, exhaustive, and careful procedure of investigation—that the given life was one of unusual, heroic "rightness," expressing a paradigmatic emanation of superhuman, divine force and the final return into this divine Source. Of course we know that for the secularized intellectual these are empty words. But perhaps it is not too much to ask of him that he take note of what is "meant."

Well, then: Thomas Aquinas was canonized on July 18, 1323, barely fifty years after his death. In connection with this we should note that, as Grabmann says,[1] Thomas seems to have been the first person canonized *for being* a theologian and teacher. The forty-two witnesses at the canonization trial had little to report concerning extraordinary acts of penance, sensational deeds, and mortifications. In fact, they seem to have been somewhat put out by this aspect of the problem: they could only repeat unanimously, again and again: Thomas had been a pure person, humble, simple, peace-loving, given to contemplation, moderate, a lover of poverty. And he himself had said repeatedly that perfection of life consists far more in inner rightness than in outer acts of asceticism.[2] One of the witnesses at the canonization trial, William of Tocco (as a young man he had been a pupil of St. Thomas and had written a detailed biography of him[3]), said that in his prayers St. Thomas had always asked for one thing only: wisdom. That is, by the by, not quite accurate. For a prayer has come down to us in which Thomas asks that it may be given him "to be serene without frivolity and mature without self-importance."[4]

Since, however, we shall be dealing with Thomas Aquinas, not so much as a man, but rather as a thinker, theologian, and above all philosopher, with Thomas the teacher and writer, the point is worth noting that even the canonization seems to have been concerned with the thinker and teacher. *Non solum virtutes, sed doctrinam etiam. . . .*[5]

Thus there began a process which was later to be confirmed and developed further when—in 1567—Thomas was declared a "doctor of the Church" and subsequently became a veritable institution. For in 1918 he was incorporated into one of the great lawbooks of history, the *Codex Juris Canonici,*[6] which directed that the priests of the Catholic Church should receive their theological and philosophical education according to the method, doctrines, and principles of Thomas Aquinas. The special title which was conferred upon Thomas, as upon almost all the other important teachers of the Middle Ages, shortly after his death—the title of *doctor communis*—has recently been taken up again with added emphasis.[7] It has been urged that Thomas, whose doctrine the Church has made her own, ought to be called *doctor communis seu universalis,* the general and universal teacher.

The enthroning of any system of thought is bound to have some undesirable results. Thus, it is only too easy for those with highly special doctrinal axes to grind to help their cause by appealing to the officially acknowledged canon, Thomas Aquinas. The same thing happens within the particular realm which has set up Karl Marx as its *doctor communis*—everyone attempts to validate his own opinion by a quotation from Marx, whether or not there is any objective justification for his use of the quotation. (Naturally, this analogy is not meant to suggest that the canonization of Marx or Lenin can be placed upon the same level as that of St. Thomas.)

I should like to forestall any misunderstanding of what I am saying here. I do not regard the special, unusual distinction conferred upon Thomas Aquinas by ecclesiastical authority as a mere chance product of certain conservative and unyielding tendencies. Nor do I consider it primarily a disciplinary measure intended to establish or preserve "intellectual unity." The Viennese theologian Albert Mitterer, for example, states that "Thomism" is "prescribed by the Church."[8] I think such phraseology extremely unfortunate, and misleading as well (as if the Church's decision were a kind of police ordinance issued solely for reasons of expediency and susceptible to abrogation or alteration). Rather, I am convinced that the pre-eminent position assigned to St. Thomas, which may now and then strike people as strange, is meaningful and necessary in terms of the subject matter itself, inherently so. Naturally, this is not to call for the sterile parroting of Thomist doctrine (the Thomas encyclical of Pius XI expressly warns against any such thing), or to press for the artificial keeping alive of those elements in Thomas which were conditioned by his times.

Mitterer insinuates that Thomas' conception of the universe was completely different from ours—false, scanty, and primitive, since he did not have the benefit of the investigations of modern science—and that this poses a dilemma for the Catholic. I must say that it has never occurred to me to extend the obligatoriness of St. Thomas' teachings to his biological doctrines. It is, moreover, generally held[9] that natural philosophy was the weakest point in the thinking of St. Thomas. He "has no heart for the task," says Gilson.[10] Rather, Thomas husbanded his intellectual powers for other subjects. Nevertheless, the very special status accorded to St. Thomas (why not to Augustine? Why not to Albertus Magnus or Bonaventura?) cannot very well mean anything but this: that in his works he succeeded in stating the whole of truth in a unique, exemplary fashion.

This very fact, however, leads to some less than commendable tendencies. For example, it strengthens the temptation to deal with Thomas in a purely derivative fashion. It favors the tendency to palm off certain theses upon Thomas, in order to give them the cachet of his authority. The "dreariness of Thomas-interpretation" may be traced to this. (The phrase is not mine, but that of the Benedictine theologian Anselm Stolz.[11])

I am not suggesting that the whole wide field of interpretation of St. Thomas is dominated by such subjective motivations. Rather, once Thomas has become an "institution," it is perfectly natural and totally unavoidable that the nature of that institution be defined. The interesting and pressing question then becomes: In what does his exemplariness, in what does his typical and unique quality consist; and above all, precisely which of his doctrines are obligatory? What, in short, is the greatness of Thomas that has made him the *doctor communis* of Christendom?

Probably it is not the "originality" of his ideas; Augustine is far more original. Perfection and originality seem in a sense mutually exclusive; what is classical is not, properly speaking, original. George Bernard Shaw in his brilliant music criticism made a remark about Mozart that can apply to Thomas as well. Shaw says: "Mozart, like Praxiteles, Raphael, Molière, Shakespeare, was no leader of a new departure or founder of a school."[12] Shaw might safely have added: "any more than was Thomas Aquinas." (I should like to recall the astonishing fact, already mentioned, that Thomas, although so great a "teacher," had no real "pupils" in the narrower sense; all his life he remained alone. Shaw continues, that one cannot say about Mozart: "Here is an entirely new vein of musical art, of which nobody ever dreamt before Mozart. . . . Anybody, almost, can make a beginning: the difficulty is to make an end—to do what cannot be bettered. . . . It is always like that. Praxiteles, Raphael and Co. have great men for their pioneers, and only fools for their followers."

Undoubtedly this sort of thing can be said less impertinently, but the essence of Shaw's observation seems to be true. What is great in the great appears to consist precisely in those qualities which rule them out as representatives of a "movement." And this is also true of Thomas. His greatness, and incidentally his timeliness, consists precisely in the fact that a real "ism" cannot properly be attached to him; that, therefore, "Thomism" cannot really exist. Not, at any rate, if we understand the term to mean a specific doctrinal tendency conditioned by polemical theses and demarcations, a system of tenets handed down from teacher to pupil, as is the case with any "school."[13] This cannot exist because the magnificent statement residing in the work of St. Thomas is far too rich; its special virtue lies in its not seeking to be anything "special." Thomas refused to be selective; he undertook the enormous task of "choosing everything." "He seeks to be faithful to the deeper intention of Saint Augustine, as well as to that of Aristotle; the deeper aim of human reason as well as of divine faith."[14] Similarly, the French Dominican Geiger, who in his much-discussed book on the concept of "participation" in Thomas Aquinas attempted to show the Platonic elements in the thinking of the alleged Aristotelian Thomas, has made the same observation: Thomas ought to have made choices but did not do so—*or il n'a pas choisi*.[15] Thomas was neither Platonist nor Aristotelian; he was both.

This peculiarity was a part of St. Thomas' basic temper, in the existential as well as the intellectual realm. How much that was so is evident in his very earliest decisions. And in these early decisions it is likewise apparent how little this refusal "to choose" had to do with neutrality or indecisiveness.

I have already mentioned that Thomas, at the age of about fifteen, had to leave the sanctuary of the Benedictine abbey of Monte Cassino, and that his flight took him to Naples, to an urban environment and a university; and that there he encountered two phenomena which were new not only to him, but also to the thirteenth century.

First of all Thomas encountered the voluntary poverty movement, the mendicant orders; and secondly he encountered, at the university, Aristotle. As a stable and entirely open-minded young man with a tremendous receptivity of soul and spirit, he encountered the two forces which were to exert a determining effect upon his own time and upon the whole future of the West as well. And Thomas embraced both with the amazing vehemence of his nature—although the drives behind these two phenomena at first appear to be contradictory. Here, then, in his first actions, I would say, there emerges the paradigmatic, the exemplary quality of the future *doctor communis:* the assimilative powers which excluded nothing, omitted nothing, which insisted that everything that is, "belongs"—for example, both the Bible and the metaphysics of Aristotle. We shall discuss this point in greater detail.

I have used the word "Bible" instead of "voluntary poverty movement." For the Biblical, the "evangelical" aspect was the most telling characteristic of that movement. Chenu employs the term *évangelisme*[16] to describe it. From a sociological point of view it was a kind of youth movement, and incidentally an urban one which flourished only on the soil of cities (Thomas would never have encountered it in Monte Cassino). It was, moreover, an "anti" movement—directed against the solid secularity of a Christianity that was making itself at home in the world economically and politically.

But the essential nature of the movement cannot be defined sociologically. The two mendicant orders were founded almost simultaneously; the Dominicans were formally confirmed as an order in 1216, the Franciscans in 1223; St. Dominic died in 1221, St. Francis of Assisi in 1226. These two foundations cannot be understood without a knowledge of the heresies from which they derived. Oversimplifying, we may say that their ancestry goes back to two movements: Catharism and Waldensianism.

The Cathars, as they called themselves (from *katharoi*, the "pure")—the medieval Cathars—were the heirs of ancient Manichaeanism, a tendency which is probably a recurrent one in human thought. The Manichees held matter and all material things to be evil, including the body, marriage, the state, visible religious institutions, and the Sacraments. The Cathars laid utmost stress upon asceticism, some even carrying this to the point of fasting themselves to death. In view of the secularization of Christianity and of the hierarchy, this movement seemed to have a good deal of right on its side. It attracted to itself a tremendous amount of misguided fervor, and the conditions of the period constantly supplied fuel to the flames.

The Waldensian movement was at first entirely orthodox, but was forced into heresy by the failure of the official Church to meet its challenge. The name stems from a merchant of Lyons called Peter Waldo who in the famine year of 1176 gave away his property and tried to live literally by the commandments of Christ, that is, by the Gospel. He gathered around him a fellowship of like-minded persons whose distinguishing marks were poverty, Bible-reading, and itinerant preaching.

These two currents mingled in a number of ways, especially in southern France, where they culminated in a massive popular movement which is usually called the Albigensian movement, after the city of Albi. All missionary efforts of the Church failed. Innocent III sent the Abbot of Cîteaux with some of his brethren to southern France to "combat heresy after the manner of St. Bernard by the power of preaching."[17] At that time, around the year 1200, the great reformer, Bernard of Clairvaux, was dead barely fifty years; yet his work had already been undone. What had happened was simple enough. A few years later the Rhineland Cistercian Caesarius of Heisterbach was to describe the process as a tragic law: discipline engenders wealth and wealth destroys the discipline.[18] At any rate, the Pope's legates descended upon the rebellious heretics. They came as judges rather than missionaries. They excommunicated, interdicted, and condemned. But that was not the worst of it. They also stripped themselves from the start of any moral advantage by appearing clothed in immoderate worldly pomp. "I met on the street," wrote the Dominican prior of Louvain, Thomas of Chantimpré,[19] whom we have already quoted, "an abbot with so many horses and so large a retinue that if I had not known him I would have taken him for a duke or count. . . . Only the addition of . . . a circlet on his brow would have been needed."

Later a new Pope, Honorius III, addressed a letter to the University of Paris calling upon the professors and students to go into the disaffected cities of southern France and conduct missions there.[20] It is highly improbable that anything of this sort was done. Moreover, it was too late, for violence had already been resorted to. The twenty-year Albigensian War had begun. Beginning as a crusade, it quickly changed—as Joseph Bernhart remarks in his papal history[21]—"in spite of the religious earnestness of many an individual knight, into a common war of conquest on the part of French barons."

At this point, then, the activity of St. Dominic began. Of Visigoth blood, born in Castile in 1170, he became subprior in the cathedral chapter of Osma. Accompanying his superior, Bishop Diego, on a journey to Rome, he naturally passed through southern France, through what may be called the "earthquake territory." He was destined not to return to his native land. Meeting the papal legate in 1206 in Montpellier, he likewise met his life's work, which he at once embraced with wholehearted passion. Dominic was then a man of thirty-five, and he would die at fifty. Yet these fifteen years could only be adequately related in the style of an Icelandic saga.

The two Spaniards, Dominic and Bishop Diego, realized that a tremendous task awaited them. They perceived that all previous attempts to win back these regions for the Church had been wrong in their whole approach. They themselves began the missionary work first of all by taking the injunction of evangelical poverty seriously, and above all by taking the heretics seriously as people sharing a common humanity with themselves.

That same year of 1206 there took place in Montréal the first real disputation in which the Albigensians did not stand like defendants before their judges but as disputants with equal rights. The two parties sought the truth according to prearranged rules of debate, one of which was the following: He who cannot prove his thesis from the Bible is to be regarded as defeated.[22]

This disputation was the germ of the Dominican Order, which from the start encountered extreme distrust within the Church. The papal legates considered this method of missionizing a folly.[23] There were, to be sure, exceptional figures who thought otherwise. One of these was Bishop Foulques of Toulouse—exceptional in many respects, for this Foulques had once been one of the most famous troubadors. Then one day he laid aside his lute, entered the Cistercian Order together with his wife and two sons, became an abbot, and, a year before the disputation of Montréal, became Bishop of Toulouse. It was he who finally obtained recognition for the Order of Preachers from Innocent III.

Dominic and Bishop Diego remained in France and established the first community of the order. A year after the disputation of Montréal, Bishop Diego died and Dominic became the sole spirit behind the dynamic movement that had so suddenly come into being. It was a movement that altogether imitated the practices of the Albigensians! "Dominic's reform movement arose out of Waldensianism."[24] "To Dominic it was clear that Waldensianism could be conquered only if its valid demands were acknowledged and carried out within the Catholic Church."[25] "Like the Waldensians, he went back to the primitive Church."[26]

Dominic's point of view was only strengthened by what he was compelled to witness, then and to the very end of his life, under his very eyes: the unspeakable cruelty of the Albigensian War. He was present at Lavaur in 1211 when, after the capture of the city, the heretics were stoned, burned, and crucified by the hundreds. But while this frenzy raged, the Dominican Order arose—although the Lateran Council had just decided that no new orders were to be confirmed. It was an order which distinguished itself in highly revolutionary fashion from the old orders. Its members had no *stabilitas loci;* they lived not in isolation but in the midst of cities. They practiced poverty in the literal sense: the poverty of beggars (begging had hitherto been forbidden to clerics[27]). Furthermore, they devoted themselves to Bible study and science; the rules of the order even stipulated that for the sake of study members could be excused from canonical prayers—a dispensation unthinkable in the Benedictine Order.[28]

But Dominic's community, which soon became known as the Order of Preachers, was likewise distinct from the Franciscan Order founded almost simultaneously by St. Francis of Assisi—even though both foundations were a response to the same challenge. In the first place, Dominic's order was an order of *priests* from the start (St. Francis was never a priest); in the second place, it was altogether unromantic in its origins, was of rational and sober complexion; in the third place, it did not reject culture and science in principle (as did St. Francis). Instead, it expressly turned its attention to the first universities of the Western world. And the university students above all, as well as their teachers, poured into the newly founded order—a remarkable and exciting fact.

With a harshness which perhaps only a Spaniard could show, Dominic sent his brethren, who were just beginning to feel at home in the community, tramping across half of Europe—without resources, without a penny, and moreover forbidden to use any form of animal transportation—to the university cities of Bologna and Paris. The community in Bologna was so miserably housed that it began to disintegrate; several of the brothers wanted to leave and had already obtained permission from the Church to enter the Cistercian Order. But then, during those first heroic years, altogether improbable events occurred (whose historicity is not open to doubt). When, for example, the brethren were assembled in Bologna to say farewell to those who were leaving the fold, one of the most famous professors of philosophy of the University of Bologna entered the room and in extreme excitement pleaded to be taken into the community of the order. This man was Roland of Cremona.[29] He became the first Dominican to receive a teaching chair at the University of Paris. Incidentally, the second teaching chair at Paris fell to the Dominicans in a similar untoward manner. The secular cleric Professor John of St. Giles was delivering a sermon on evangelical poverty at the Dominican monastery of St. Jacques. In the course of the sermon he suddenly stopped and asked for the habit of the order.

Events of this sort could not but make a bit of a sensation in the university. Among the papers of the second general of the Dominican Order, Jordan of Saxony, we find in a letter from Paris of the year 1226: "During the first four weeks of my presence twenty-one brothers entered the order; six of these are doctors of the Faculty of Arts."[30] During the winter semester of 1235–36 he presided over the induction of seventy-two scholars. It was like a conflagration. When Dominic died in 1221, exhausted by fifteen years of the most strenuous labors, there were nuclei of the order in Spain, France, Italy, Germany, Hungary, England, Sweden, and Denmark—a total of more than thirty monasteries.

We have reviewed the events and atmosphere of these founding years in order to understand the auspices under which Thomas, not two decades after the death of St. Dominic, met the Dominicans in Naples, and what his own entrance into the order must have meant. Here was an order dominated on the one hand by the passion for the enunciation of the truth (in his first *summa,* the *Summa Against the Pagans,* Thomas calls this the *propositum nostrae intentionis,* the aim that matters to us[31]—enunciation of truth in such a way that the truth reveals itself as itself and by itself to the opponent in particular). Its other drive was evangelical. It embodied the same radical tendency which had fired Peter Waldo and its own founder Dominic—a radical return to the Bible and a renewed dedication to the ideal of poverty. This last is an element which is also present in the *doctrine* of St. Thomas, but which is often completely repressed. We cannot deal with it here expressly and in detail. But it is important to know that these elements played a part in the inner life of Thomas, and have a place in his philosophy. "Evangelical perfection" is a concept that occurs many times in Thomas.[32] "Evangelical perfection consists in the imitation of Christ; but Christ was poor not only in his desire, but also in reality [*realiter*]"—this is a sentence from one of the polemical pamphlets written in behalf of the voluntary poverty movement.[33]

But the Biblical element counts for far more in the work of St. Thomas, though the same is not true for scholasticism generally. The *Summa theologica* contains three extensive tracts on Biblical theology,[34] which at that time was an innovation. It was something new for Thomas himself, and a far cry from the "systematic" theology of the commentaries on the *Sentences.* In this Thomas was showing the influence of the voluntary poverty movement. Thomas drew upon Biblical example to justify the incursions of the mendicant orders into the fields of preaching and pastoral care: "There are to be found [in the parish clergy] only very few, *paucissimi,* who know Holy Scripture—although the proclaimer of the Word of God must be conversant with Holy Scripture."[35] Even while Thomas was writing his commentary on Aristotle's *Physics* in the Dominican monastery of St. Jacques in Paris, others of the same community were engaged on the mighty labor of the first Bible corrections and the first Bible concordance.

We stress this preoccupation with the Bible in order to show the other end of the arc which Thomas undertook to span. The two ends belong together. If we consider only the one end, the attempt to imitate the guiding image provided by the Gospels, we would regard Thomas as only a mendicant friar, a phenomenon of significance only within the Church. The picture must be supplemented by the other side of Thomas: the highly realistic and secular aspect of him which turned to Aristotle. Yet we would sadly misunderstand what this "Aristotelianism" (in quotation marks!) is all about if we did not see it as permeated and interpenetrated by the apparently alien and even opposed element of a strongly evangelical Christianity. It is in this light, then, that we must speak of St. Thomas' encounter with Aristotle.

III

The intellectual dynamics of the early thirteenth century was, we have said, determined chiefly by two forces, both revolutionary and both of tremendous vitality: on the one hand the radical evangelism of the voluntary poverty movement, which rediscovered the Bible and made it the guide to Christian doctrine and Christian life; and on the other hand the no less fierce urge to investigate, on the plane of pure natural philosophy, the reality that lay before men's eyes. This latter movement in the direction of a hitherto unknown and novel "worldliness" found ammunition in the complete works of Aristotle, which were at that time just beginning to be discovered.

Both movements contained within themselves sufficient explosive force to shatter the whole structure of medieval Christianity's intellectual order. Both appeared in extremist form—theologically speaking, in the form of heresies. The remarkable thing about St. Thomas, who was exposed to these two intellectual currents while he was still a student at Naples, is that he recognized and accepted the rightness of both approaches; that he identified himself with both; that he affirmed both, although they seemed mutually opposed to one another; and that he attempted to incorporate both in his own spiritual and intellectual life. The paradigmatic, the exemplary quality of St. Thomas is, as we have said, contained precisely in his refusal to "choose" between the two extreme possibilities. Instead he "chose" both—and did so not by merely tacking one onto the other in a mechanical fashion, but by grasping and demonstrating their inherent compatibility; in fact, by showing the necessity for fusing these apparently contradictory and mutually exclusive approaches to the world.

So far we have spoken only of one end of the arc which Thomas undertook to span and manipulate. We have spoken of the evangelical and Biblical element, of Thomas' casting back to the *Ecclesia primitiva*—as it was represented in the largely heretical and destructive voluntary poverty movement, and as it was subsequently tamed in the mendicant orders. What had led Thomas into the Dominican Order as a youthful student was, *first,* his yearning for the guiding light of evangelical Christianity —his love for the ideal of poverty. In the canonization trial the witnesses particularly emphasized this: that all his life, Thomas had been a *praecipuus paupertatis amator.*

A telling part of the picture is the fact that Thomas, in his restless career which kept him constantly on the move from assignment to assignment, between Naples, Paris, Cologne, Rome, and Toulouse, made all these journeys on foot—just as did Albertus Magnus who, as superior of the German chapters of the order, imposed harsh penances upon his priors and brethren if any of them dared to use a mount. He himself tramped through almost all of Europe, from southern France to the amber coast of East Prussia, and from Paris to Hungary (a feat which earned him, as Bishop of Regensburg, the nickname of "The Clog"). This too may be added on the subject of voluntary poverty: when Thomas wrote the *Summa Against the Pagans* he did not even have enough paper at hand, and had to use small scraps. So at least we read in the proceedings of the canonization trial.[1]

The *second* thing which brought Thomas into the Order of Preachers was his passion for teaching. Teaching does not consist in a man's making public talks on the results of his meditations, even if he does so *ex cathedra* before a large audience. Teaching in the real sense takes place only when the hearer is reached—not by dint of some personal magnetism or verbal magic, but rather, when the truth of what is said reaches the hearer as truth. Real teaching takes place only when its ultimate result—which must be intended from the start—is achieved: when the hearer is "taught." And being taught is something else again from being carried away, and something else again from being dominated by another's intellect. Being taught means to perceive that what the teacher has said is true and valid, and to perceive why this is so. Teaching therefore presupposes that the hearer is sought out where he is to be found.

Thus teaching implies proceeding from the existing position and disposition of the hearer. Nor can that position be determined abstractly in advance, or fixed once and for all; it must be located in its own historical context, determined concretely for what it is. The hearer's counterarguments must be taken seriously and the elements of truth in them recognized—for aside from the products of feeblemindedness or intellectual gamesmanship, there are no entirely false opinions. The teacher, then, must proceed from what is valid in the opinions of the hearer to the fuller and purer truth as he, the teacher, understands it.

That is the nature of teaching as Thomas understood it. In this procedure, therefore, the hearer has an absolute right to "speak up," even if he does not actually take the floor. The teacher must give him the floor within the framework of his own lecture. Here, then, is the old Socratic-Platonic conception at work: that truth develops only in dialogue, in conversation. This, precisely, was what Dominic had striven for when, shocked by the violent methods being used against the Albigensians and convinced of the utter futility of a merely authoritative, merely judicial mode of establishing truth—the very opposite of "teaching"—he replaced interrogation by dialogue between equals in the famous disputation at Montréal.

At this point, however, a terrible matter must be mentioned, one which is diametrically opposed to everything that we have said about Dominic's and Thomas' own ethics of teaching and the propagation of truth. This terrible matter is called the Inquisition. It cannot be passed over because the Inquisition—precisely during the lifetime of Thomas Aquinas—very directly affected the first generations of the Dominican Order. It represents, moreover, a taint and a disgrace that cannot be wiped out by any attempts at "historical" explanation.

It was a Dominican (Ferrier) who, at the very time that Thomas was entering the order, set up the first In-

33

quisitional tribunals in France. It was another Dominican, Robert le Bougre, known as "the Scoundrel," who in May of the year that Thomas arrived in Naples (1239), had one hundred and eighty Cathars, together with their bishop, burned in Champagne. Even at this early period Dominican monasteries were stormed on this account.[2] "Inquisitional trial," as we well know, meant threats, coercion, application of force—not, moreover, in war, but in carrying out the defense of doctrines. Obviously this is the very opposite of propagation of truth by teaching, which Dominic, the founder of the order, and Thomas Aquinas stood for.

What can we say? Naturally, it is quite impossible, within the framework of these lectures, even to attempt a full account of the Inquisition. And as far as passing judgment is concerned, I do not know whether there is anyone, even given a full knowledge of all the facts, who would be capable of a wholly just judgment. On the whole we must no doubt speak of an unjustifiable, fearful aberration which leaves us horrified and mystified—although we understand that such things become possible as soon as the spiritual power joins hands with the secular power (as has happened in the West ever since the days of Constantine). But the perplexing aspect of this is that we also cannot wish the two realms to have nothing whatsoever to do with one another. Wherever a social order, or rather the power that preserves this social order, sees the foundations of the order shaken, endangered not by plans for overthrow but by ideas, there looms on the horizon the possibility of an Inquisition; in this the Middle Ages were no different from today, whether we speak of modern Russia or of modern America. It is plain that this is an everlasting temptation and danger.

In 1230 or 1231, ten years after the death of Dominic,

34

Pope Gregory IX assigned to the Dominican Order, of all institutions, the task of providing Inquisitors for the trials of heretics. This same Dominican Order, it should be remembered, had been founded out of awareness that the only way to deal with the Waldensian-Albigensian movement was for the Church itself to recognize and carry out the heretics' justified demands. If we wish to appraise this papal act correctly, we must consider its connection with a number of other matters. For it was essentially a *countermeasure*. Countering what? Countering a number of things.

In the first place it was directed against the Emperor, or rather against the legal practice initiated by Frederick II, the supposedly "modern" and "liberal" Hohenstaufen, of having heretics tracked down by officials of the state—thus leaving the primary condemnation of heretics to men who were ill-equipped to deal with the problem.

Secondly, the papal ordinance was meant to counter the vagaries of "popular feeling"—in which irrational elements have always been mingled with highly rational aims governed by private vengeance and enmities. The sources state with one accord that the people—one might also say "the masses," if not "the mob," "the rabble"—always demanded the harshest, cruelest measures and would have preferred to inflict these themselves, in acts of savage lynch law. *Inquisitio* means investigation—and this precisely was the Pope's concern: a real investigation, a judicial procedure, instead of outright lynching, instead of simplistic police brutality. When we find one historian describing the introduction of the Inquisition as a "step forward in juristic theory,"[3] we must understand him in this sense. At any rate, here is a new possible explanation for the fact that the Dominicans should have been the ones chosen for this assignment. The intention was to put a stop to the violence of which the Albigensians had been victims for close to thirty years. But this attempt to alleviate an evil led to fresh evils. It led above all to something that ultimately perverted into its opposite the original intention of the order's founder.

Thomas Aquinas, too, apparently could not raise himself above his times. In the *Summa theologica*[4] he poses the question of whether heretics can be endured, tolerated; that is, whether it is right to let them go their way. And his answer is that heretics can *not* be tolerated. If it was just to condemn counterfeiters to death (and this is a factor which must always be borne in mind: the general harshness of judicial penalties in those times), then surely it was necessary to put to death those who had committed the far worse crime of counterfeiting the faith.[5] For eternal salvation must be regarded as greater than temporal property, and the welfare of all must be regarded as greater than the welfare of an individual.

This principle, of course, says nothing about the *procedure* by which guilt was to be determined—and *that* was the area of the most terrible abuses. Nevertheless, no Christian of our own times can possibly agree with the *doctor communis* on this point. (Though we may well ask: On what grounds do we find it impossible to agree? Obviously not on the grounds of being a "modern" man! When we think of the most "modern" practices in the realm of contemporary "ideological terrorism," we find that we can scarcely lay claim to any moral superiority over the Middle Ages.) What is so utterly incomprehensible in the case of St. Thomas is that in his *Treatise on the Faith* he states quite clearly what is perfectly obvious: No one can be forced to believe; people can do many things under compulsion, but the one thing they cannot do is believe.

As far as the procedures of investigation are concerned,

there is among St. Thomas' *opuscula* one written during his last years, entitled *On Secrecy*. This is not, as it happens, an essay composed by Thomas alone; it is a collection of answers to questions, a symposium in which he participated with seven others.

One of the questions posed was the following: Assuming that one man accuses another of a fault which he, the accuser, alone knows of, or which he cannot prove: in such a case may the Superior himself launch an inquiry; or may he order the accused to tell the truth before the assembly of the brethren; and is the accused thereby obligated to confess his fault to the Superior?[6] Let us transpose this question into the terminology and the atmosphere of contemporary investigative procedures directed at "ideological deviations"; and if we consider how, in East and West, use is made of the lie detector, secret tape-recording, television surveillance, and special drugs, we see how extremely timely this subject of "secrecy" is in connection with totalitarian practices and with the whole matter of "Inquisitions."

Let us, furthermore, view this question which was put to St. Thomas in connection with the usual notions we have formed of the "Inquisition" and "coercion of conscience" in the thirteenth century. What answer would we expect to find, nowadays and at that time? Certainly not, it seems to me, the answer Thomas actually gives. It reads as follows: "The Superior may *not* so order [that the accused should confess]; if he does, he sins gravely. And the accused is not required to expose himself; rather, he may say: Let the accuser prove what he has said; otherwise I demand a judgment [against him] for defamation. The accused may answer something along these lines, or else he may simply keep silent. *Quia in occultis non est homo iudex,* man is not appointed the judge of what is hidden."[7]

This reply scarcely accords with the idea that this same Thomas was an advocate of the Inquisition. I myself know no solution to the paradox. But it is important to take note of this paradox. It appears all the sharper when we see how Thomas as a writer and teacher handled the opinions of opponents. For he shows not a trace of dictatorial or magisterial attitude. It can happen to anyone reading, say, the *Summa Against the Pagans,* that he will come unsuspectingly upon a chapter in which Thomas expounds the arguments of the opposite camp; if theological matters are under discussion, these arguments may well be heretical; yet the reader will almost be inclined to consider the arguments irrefutable—so entirely without bias does Thomas present them. He himself brings to light their force with a persuasiveness which the opponent himself might well have envied. Here Thomas completely fulfilled the dialogue character of his work, the quality of a dialogue between persons who respect one another. That does not mean that each opinion is right; but it does mean that each side has the right to formulate his argument and that each is obligated to listen to the other. Truth must be brought to bear in and for itself, with its own inherent strength, and not by means of an adventitious force. This special quality of St. Thomas' mode of thinking and speaking, which is evidenced throughout his entire works, and especially in the polemical writings, continues in pure form the impetus which originally led to the foundation of the Dominican Order. And it was Thomas' inner affinity with that drive, in addition to his decision to live a life of evangelical poverty, that led him to enter that order.

Now, however, it is time to speak of the second element which Thomas, with his tremendous powers of affirmation and assimilation, likewise embraced. This other end of the arc is summed up by the name "Aristotle."

Virtually nowhere else in the West was it possible to encounter Aristotle so intensely and so comprehensively as in the city of Naples. In the first place, Sicily, to which Naples of course belonged at that time, had always been a border area and transfer point between East and West. At the court of the Norman kings, and later at the Hohenstaufen court, foreign elements of both Greek and Arabic origin were present in the most natural way—as neighbors are always present in border areas. Under the Hohenstaufen emperors the city of Palermo was a kind of translation center. Frederick II brought the mysterious Michael Scot (Michael Scotus) to Palermo as court astrologer; and this savant, who had been educated in Oxford, and had learned Arabic in Toledo and already made translations from the Arabic while still in Spain, went to work (around 1230) translating Averroës, the commentator on Aristotle, into Latin. He directed a whole team of translators. It also appears that he brought with him or recommended the Irishman Peter of Hibernia, who subsequently became young Thomas' teacher. . . . The second reason why a student at the University of Naples could steep himself in the work of Aristotle was the fact that this purely state university, which was keenly aware of its independence from the Church, flagrantly flouted Rome's official ban against Aristotle.

The *Logic* of Aristotle had been accepted textbook matter in Western schools since the times of Boethius. In the twelfth century, by various adventurous routes—translations not directly from Greek into Latin, but from Arabic into Latin, the Arabic versions themselves resting upon Syrian translations—the works of Aristotle dealing with natural philosophy, together with his books on metaphysics, ethics, and psychology, became known in the West almost all at once. This meant a good deal more than the addition of a few books to the curriculum. Suddenly a totally new, rounded, coherent view of the world was pitted against another more or less coherent traditional view.

What added to the excitement was that these novel Aristotelian ideas were not entirely strange. Something had been gestating within Western Christendom of the second millennium and was practically on the verge of seeing the light—a view of the universe and life that greatly resembled the Aristotelian viewpoint. This fellow Aristotle "suited" Western Christendom of around 1200 uncannily well; he offered to the Christian world the possibility of understanding itself. And so the result is not too surprising: this new thing, "like a wildly roaring torrent" (as Grabmann, who is inclined to avoid exaggeration and is usually very temperate in his phraseology, expresses it), threatened to sweep away the dams and levees of tradition.[8] Nor is it surprising that some men should have been concerned, afraid that the coherence of tradition might be shattered by the assault of radicals infatuated by the new ideas. It is perfectly understandable that in their concern for the totality of truth their first act should have been a defensive one. After all, it was too much to expect that any man would emerge with the enormous powers of assimilation needed to establish some kind of "co-existence" between the new doctrines, no matter whether they were a thousand times true and valid, and the Old Truth.

It must be said that the ecclesiastical warnings, restrictions, and prohibitions were a hopeless business from the start; and it appears that the ecclesiastical authorities were not entirely unaware of this. There is something strangely lackadaisical about these ordinances, which were only spottily enforced. The University of Toulouse, for example, though also an ecclesiastical institution, in its efforts to recruit students openly advertised that in Toulouse it was permissible to do what was forbidden in Paris—that is, to study Aristotle.[9] The result of this publicity, however, was that in 1245 the ban against Aristotle was expressly extended to Toulouse.

The year 1245 was the same year that Thomas set out for Paris; he had already completed his studies of Aristotle at Naples. And in Paris, despite the persistence of the ban, Aristotle was unquestionably in the curriculum. We possess Thomas' own copies, dating from his first year of study under Albertus Magnus, of lectures on Aristotle's *Nicomachean Ethics*. In 1263 Rome issued a reiteration of the prohibition of Aristotle. But in St. Thomas' first book, *De ente et essentia,* written almost ten years before (1254), the first chapter opens with a quotation from the *Metaphysics*. Moreover, Aristotle is not quoted as just any author, but is alluded to by his honorary title of *"the* Philosopher."

At this same period Albert was writing his great commentary on Aristotle—"under the eyes of the popes," Grabmann says;[10] probably this means in defiance of the popes. I confess that I do not fully understand how this state of affairs was possible, either for the popes or for these wholly papal-minded monks. It is also baffling that, as Grabmann says, the commentaries on Aristotle by Albert and Thomas "practically abrogated"[11] the Church's ruling. Probably such inconsistencies reflect the historical cross-currents: on the one hand the elementary process of assimilating Aristotle was begun and concluded within the span of barely a generation; on the other hand the Church took understandable and no doubt necessary measures to preserve the continuity of tradition in spite of the new ideas coming to the fore.

In 1366, when the papal legates once more surveyed the

curriculum and examination schedules of the University of Paris, they insisted that any candidate for the academic degree of Licentiate in Philosophy at Paris must be familiar with all the works of Aristotle. And this obtained deep into the sixteenth and seventeenth centuries. When Luther began teaching in Wittenberg, he delivered lectures on Aristotle's *Nicomachean Ethics*—which did not deter him from later speaking of the philosopher as "Foolistotle" (Narristoteles).

It was, then, at the earliest stage of this incorporation of Aristotle into Christianity's philosophical and theological world view that Thomas, in Naples, attended Peter of Hibernia's lectures on Aristotle. This Irishman, of whose works we retain a disputation in the presence of King Manfred, was an example of the new type of university professor, "more modern"[12] than the authors of the earlier commentaries on the *Sentences* and *summas*. His modernity consisted in his primarily philosophical interests, and his de-emphasizing of theology.[13] This means, therefore, that Thomas made his first acquaintance with Aristotelianism not in a moderate but in an extreme and altogether dangerous form. It becomes all the more astonishing that Thomas nevertheless undertook to assimilate this material apparently so incompatible with the radically Biblical and evangelical temper of the voluntary poverty movement, and to demonstrate that the two directions actually belonged together. To understand this we must first of all try to see what the acceptance of Aristotle meant to Thomas personally. For what it meant to him was different from what it meant to his teacher, Peter of Hibernia. And it had nothing to do with "Aristotelianism."

IV

The simple fact is that those who have dubbed Thomas with the epithet "Aristotelian" have not hit the mark. This is the reason why the first modern efforts to open up the world of St. Thomas—which date from about 1890—failed. Yet they established an image of Thomas which prevailed for a long time—an image which has in fact prevailed to the present day. One of the first complete systematic accounts of St. Thomas' basic philosophical ideas, a book which serves as a text even now, bears the title *Elementa philosophiae Aristotelico-Thomisticae*.[1]

But why should it seriously matter to us today, after seven hundred years, beyond our interest in the purely historical aspects of the subject, that Thomas was "the founder of the Christian Aristotelianism of the Middle Ages"?[2] Certainly it was not for this alone that Thomas has been pronounced the *doctor communis* of Christendom.

But to repeat—from a purely historical point of view, too, it is a misinterpretation of what really happened to imagine that young Thomas turned to Aristotelianism because it had become modish and that he thus became an "Aristotelian." This notion literally obstructed any real understanding of Thomas for decades[3]—until in recent years it was energetically pointed out that Plato too, Augustine too, the Neo-Platonist Dionysius Areopagita too, are very much present and effective in the work of St. Thomas, and that Thomas himself was not unaware of their presence. Thomas frequently defends Plato against Aristotle; he points out that Aristotle, in his polemics, often did not consider the substance of what Plato said, the *veritas occulta*,[4] but only the superficial phrasing, the *sonus verborum*.[5] The doctrine of Ideas, the conception of the Creation as following prototypes living within the divine Logos[6]—this central Platonic concept was something that Thomas never abandoned. And a tally of the works of St. Thomas has turned up almost seventeen hundred quotations from Dionysius Areopagita.

This will astonish only those who regard intellectual history as a succession of "isms" that replace one another. But of course it is not so. In the history of Western thought Plato, for example, could never be "displaced" or replaced by Aristotle;[7] in fact, the former was never an obstacle in the way of the latter. Gilson has convincingly demonstrated that. The Christian West's encounter with Plato, as it took form during the first millennium, was wholly different in structure from its encounter with Aristotle. The encounter with Plato was an encounter of two religious modes of thought; but the encounter with Aristotle was the encounter between religion and philosophy.[8]

The question, then, is what it meant to Thomas when he turned to Aristotle.

We find Thomas giving us ever new shades of the fundamental Aristotelian position. Aristotle, he says, refuses to withdraw from the realities present to the senses, refuses to be distracted from those things that are evident to the eyes.[9] And Thomas himself emphatically accepted this principle. Here was the decisive turn to concreteness, to the empirical reality of the world. Those things evident to the senses, which can be seen, heard, tasted, smelled, and touched, are to be taken as realities in their own right, standing on their own ground—not as mere reflections, shadows, not as mere symbols of something else, something invisible, spiritual, otherworldly. The visible, and sight itself, the perceptions of the senses and the power of perception—all that is now affirmed and acknowledged to be valid in itself. Which means that the physical world of material reality, *within* man himself also, the body, the

44

senses and what the senses grasp—is all to be taken seriously in a manner hitherto unknown.

Several reasons can be offered as to why the world view of Aristotle, above all his theories of nature, his theories of the human soul, and his metaphysics, should have made the conquest they did. One reason, of course, is the immediately obvious intellectual superiority of their proponent. When a new idea emerges which explains and illuminates phenomena better than earlier ideas, it exerts an irresistible force. And Aristotle was after all not just some writer who had significant things to say. Aristotle was like a phenomenon of nature: a personification of intellectual energy of elemental power, within whose field of radiation fundamental problems and situations seemed to be clarified of their own accord. This has been said again and again in various ways. "The intellect in its highest manifestation," says Goethe of him.[10] And John Henry Newman: "He has told us the meaning of our own words and ideas, before we were born. In many subject matters, to think correctly is to think like Aristotle."[11] It is quite understandable that around 1200, men in the West should decide that God had imparted to the great Greek some of His own wisdom, had endowed him with miraculous powers, and at last had taken him to Himself in a pillar of light.[12] But it need scarcely be said that nothing of this sort is to be found in Thomas. For Thomas was anything but a participant in the "excessive cult of Aristotle"[13] which had become a fad in his time. Grabmann remarks that he has found no evaluations of Aristotle at all in the works of Thomas.[14] This very restraint, to be sure, is in keeping with the Aristotelian style.

We have already suggested a second reason for the fascination exerted by the works of Aristotle. In the bosom of Western Christendom of the second millennium a world view was already preparing, independently, which was much akin to the Aristotelian world view, an element that quickly made common cause with the other. This element arising of its own accord in Western Christendom has been called the "Hohenstaufen spirit." The whole era of the Hohenstaufens, it has been said, must be understood as a rebellion against the old Augustinian-Cluniac doctrine of the inferiority of the natural world—that is, against contempt for the world. "The whole of the courtly, chivalric culture restores its due to the world and the here-and-now."[15] The same author states that Thomas Aquinas' Aristotelian cosmology was literally "the subsequent philosophical justification for the attitude which Hohenstaufen poetry and the Hohenstaufen spirit had long since assumed."[16] This statement is probably far too simplistic, where it is not downright wrong. We cannot say that older Christendom was identified absolutely with "contempt for the world." On the other hand it is true that Albertus Magnus, a Swabian nobleman, was related by blood to the Hohenstaufens; and we have already mentioned that Thomas likewise was closely connected with Hohenstaufen circles through his father and brother, who were among the courtiers of Frederick II.

But probably we must say that the poetry, the spirit, and the philosophy all together were rooted in some deeper soil—soil in which religious convictions are also formed. There is much to be said for Chenu's conjecture: that what Aristotle brought so vividly to light for the minds of those decades, and what they primarily saw in his work, was not so much natural reason as nature itself, the natural reality of the universe.[17] This element, evidently, was what so powerfully agitated and fascinated the "younger generation." I have mentioned that the University of Toulouse for a time recruited students by advertising that the study of Aristotle was permitted there, though banned in Paris. As it happens, we possess the text of one such bit of propaganda which expressly mentions the *Physics* of Aristotle: "The books on nature, *libri naturales,* which are forbidden in Paris, are available to anyone here who has the will to penetrate more deeply into the innermost heart of nature."[18]

Thomas himself, in his first great work, the *Summa Against the Pagans,* put it this way: the theological point of view does not consider fire "as such," insofar as it is fire, but insofar as the sovereignty of God is represented in it and insofar as it is in some sense referred to God.[19] (This is, as I have said, an *early* definition of theology; later Thomas phrases it differently.) Such denaturalization of the natural world sooner or later had to become intolerable; it is simply impossible to live a healthy and human life in a world populated exclusively by symbols. And by around 1200 the moment had come for Christendom, out of what may be termed a purely vital reaction, to grow sick and tired of seeing and denominating the world in that way. What the twelfth century lacked, and craved, was the concrete reality *beneath* this world of symbols.[20] It was altogether logical that in the midst of the Christian West itself this irrepressible longing for the hard metal and the resistant substance of "real reality," so long submerged, must at last burst forth as a mighty, many-voiced, and enthusiastic assent toward the Aristotelian cosmology, as soon as that whole complex of ideas about the universe hove in sight.

I have said that theology and philosophy here encountered one another—philosophy in the sense that Thomas defined it in that chapter of the *Summa Against the Pagans,*[21] as a mode of seeing things as they are *in themselves, secundum quod huiusmodi sunt:* fire as fire and not as a

47

mere symbol of divine sovereignty. What emerged in this early Aristotelianism was a completely elemental outburst of "worldliness," antagonistic toward the spiritualistic symbolism which had hitherto governed the tone of Christian cosmology and biology. And as was very soon to become apparent, that worldliness was naturally linked with the peril of complete secularization.

Such, then, was the situation which Thomas found around 1240 at the University of Naples—or rather, in whose midst he could not forbear to plunge. And the magnificent part of it all is that he succeeded in uniting this hearty worldliness with the radicality of the evangelical spirit, which has always rather tended toward negation of the world, or at least toward unworldliness.

Sure enough, the charge of worldliness was soon raised by conservative Christians. "They arrogated to themselves divine wisdom, although worldliness is far more native to their minds"—so we may read in a polemic against Thomas and Albert. Whereupon Thomas responded: "They hold a plainly false opinion who say that in regard to the truth of religion it does not matter what a man thinks about the Creation so long as he has the correct opinion concerning God. An error concerning the Creation ends as false thinking about God."[22]

In such a sentence as this Thomas makes plain that he was not reacting simply out of instinct, however much he may have been in the sway of the "Hohenstaufen spirit." It was not in the spirit of chivalry that he found the symbolic deconcretization of the world of sense intolerable; it was as a theologian that Thomas cast his choice for the worldliness represented by the works of Aristotle. What is truly exciting about this choice is the reason Thomas gives for it. His turning to Aristotle was a process of recognition, not of "acceptance" of something foreign, Greek

48

and "pagan." In Aristotle's fundamental attitude toward the universe, in his affirmation of the concrete and sensuous reality of the world, Thomas recognized something entirely his own, belonging to himself as a Christian because it had been present from the very beginnings of Christianity. To put it in a nutshell, this element was the same as the Christian affirmation of Creation.

We shall have to discuss this point further: that the reception of Aristotle in the thirteenth century was not merely the result of "a choice between rival philosophies," but was a theological act, the work of a theology in full possession of its faith[23] (though also a theology that had not yet become a mere special branch of scholarship jealously fencing off its particular area); the action of a theology which was not yet separated from the world, its conditions, its perspectives, its procedures, its culture.[24] We shall, I say, discuss this later. At this point in our considerations the chief thing is to realize as vividly as possible what it signifies that Thomas, while still a young man, accomplished so unique a task: that of joining these two apparently incompatible decisions (*for* the "Gospel" and *for* "Aristotle") and creating, intellectually and existentially, a foundation upon which the whole orderly structure of the Christian world view could be raised, a structure which continues to serve us to this day, and seems to have a timeless durability. For Thomas, both decisions signified a turning point in his life. And he adhered to both decisions to the day of his death. Even toward the close of his life, in 1270, he published a polemic glorifying the evangelical ideal of the Dominican Order. He did not begin his commentaries on the writings of Aristotle until the last decade of his life (around 1266), and when he finally ceased writing, a number of these commentaries were left uncompleted.

A few more remarks are in order, to cast light on the significance of this lifelong concentration upon Aristotle. This endless quoting from and commenting on Aristotle did *not* mean that Thomas regarded Aristotle as the absolute authority. And the usual talk about "influences" and "dependence," in which history books abound, misses the point completely. Yet what do the thousands of quotations from Aristotle in the works of St. Thomas (in the first twelve *quaestiones* of the *Summa theologica* there are fifty-five such quotations) mean if not that he regarded Aristotle as an authority?

Let us remember that a quotation can have several uses.[25] It can be mere ornament—when, for example, its diction is specially elegant. It can be intended historically. But it is not for either of these reasons that the Communists, say, cite Karl Marx—although in this realm, too, there are infinite nuances: protection, camouflage, deception, provocation. In the main, however, the Communist world cites Karl Marx as an authority. In other words, something is true because Marx said it. We contend that St. Thomas does not cite Aristotle in this sense. But what, you may well ask, is the meaning of the constantly recurring formula: "As the Philosopher [Aristotle] says," or *sicut patet per Philosophum?* Is not the implication: "He" said it and therefore it is true?

The answer is no—it does not mean that. *Sicut patet per Philosophum* must be rendered: as has been made clear by Aristotle. Not because it is Aristotle who said it, but because he said it in a way that throws light on the problem—that is why it is so. (The fact that the "he" is Aristotle is, to be sure, no accident.) It is so because it is true. A writer who quotes in this manner is not really quoting an authority; he is not tying himself to the author's apron strings. On the other hand he does not hesitate to cite an author if it seems to him that this author is right and has contrived to express the truth in exemplary fashion. He takes the liberty of concurring with someone who, he believes, has told the truth.

I do not deny that there are also a great many quotations from Aristotle in Thomas which are intended solely as ornament, or even as confirmations of the saint's own exposition. But what I do venture to assert is this: Thomas never presents a quotation from Aristotle with the implication that the statement is valid because Aristotle made it. Thomas very often takes issue with some opinion of Aristotle's. He never assumed that the doctrine of Aristotle was invariably compatible with Christian doctrine. This attitude was quite prevalent among medieval Aristotelians; Thomas himself was never of this number; we find him speaking of "those who vainly endeavor to prove that Aristotle said nothing against the faith. . . ."[26] But above and beyond all that, as is well known, Thomas stated outright that the argument from authority is, in itself and quite generally, the weakest of all arguments.[27] To attempt to prove something on the basis of authority is to prove nothing, he says.[28]

We have, however, not quoted these statements in context. Thomas qualifies them. The argument from authority, he says, is the weakest argument insofar as *human* knowledge is in question; where its basis is divine revelation, it possesses supreme power.[29] Thus Thomas fully acknowledges the authority whose word is valid because it comes from this source, irrespective of whether we are able to check on its truth and validity. All true tradition leads back to this superhuman source; the *traditum,* what has been handed down, is valid *because* it ultimately derives from the Word of God.[30] This very acceptance of an absolutely valid authority and an absolutely valid tradition, this very restriction, makes for freedom and an unbiased attitude toward all other historically encounterable "traditions" and authorities, whether their names happen to be Aristotle or Marx or Heidegger or St. Thomas. Philosophical arguments, Thomas says,[31] are valid "not because of the authority of those who state them, but because of the reasoning of what is stated," *non . . . propter auctoritatem dicentium, sed propter rationem dictorum.*

There is something else closely connected with this: namely, that Thomas in his lifelong labors of interpreting Aristotle was ultimately not concerned with the historical author named Aristotle, nor with an accurate reconstruction of his doctrine. This last statement must at once be clarified, lest it be misunderstood. It is true that Thomas endeavored, in a manner highly unusual for the thirteenth century, to discover Aristotle's real meaning. His commentaries on Aristotle remain to this day among the few congenial commentaries which truly cast light upon Aristotle's doctrines—this in spite of the mediocre translations upon which Thomas had to rely, and although he himself scarcely knew Greek, and although, in the case of the *Metaphysics,* he had no inkling that the book was not planned as a unit and cast in one mold, as it were, but was a miscellaneous collection of very different pieces. Nevertheless, the ultimate intent of St. Thomas' interpretation of Aristotle aimed at something beyond Aristotle. "He sticks to his text, it is true, and he wants to understand it—but not as a scholar who indulges in the historical reproduction of a system belonging to the past; rather, as a seeker, who wishes to find in it a witness for the truth."[32]

What interests Thomas in Aristotle, then, is not Aristotle, but the truth. He is not primarily concerned with "what others have thought"—this is his own phraseology, and to be found, moreover, in a commentary on Aristotle which yet obviously aims at finding out what Aristotle did think.[33] For ultimately he is interested not in what Aristotle thought but in "how the truth of things stands."[34] Naturally this does not mean that Thomas considered it possible or permissible to falsify the real meaning of Aristotle where, say, it runs counter to Christian doctrine, or even to conceal that meaning. This last was, for example, seriously proposed by Bonaventura.[35] Because of Aristotle's great influence, he argued, any false elements in Aristotle's teachings ought to be passed over in silence. In contrast, Thomas advocated the following course: We will say that Aristotle teaches exactly what he does teach; but we will determine whether he really teaches it, and above all we will not conclude from the mere fact that he taught it that it is true. "Even if it contradicts the truth, the *intentio Aristotelis,* what Aristotle meant, ought not to be concealed," he says.[36] And he adds: "Incidentally, I do not see that the manner in which one interprets the sentences of the Philosopher ought to have anything to do with the doctrine of faith."

To be sure, Thomas would never have concurred with the opinion of a contemporary of his who can with justice be called an "Aristotelian," his colleague at the University of Paris, Siger of Brabant. Siger maintained that one must "rather seek to discover the meaning of the Philosopher than the truth."[37] "The medieval philosophers were . . . not interested in Greek philosophy in purely historical terms. . . . The historical Aristotle was for them only the truth which he himself derived from his principles, not also the truth which his principles were capable of sustaining. The historical Aristotle was for them Aristotle in all his grandeur, but also with all his limitations. The same was true for Plato. The medieval philosophers, in studying Aristotle and Plato, wished to know all those things and only those things which were true. Where the truths of these philosophers were not complete, they asked themselves how to complete them."[38]

There is an enormous difference between this attitude and that usually held nowadays and which we consider the sole possible and responsible attitude toward "sources." For the student especially, that difference is of vital importance. Anyone who asks Thomas his opinion receives a reply which makes perfectly clear what he, Thomas, considers to be the truth—even when his reply is couched in the form of a quotation from Aristotle. But if we are asked our opinion, we reply with historically documented quotations which may reveal a good many things—for example, how widely read we are—but fail to reveal one thing alone: what we ourselves hold to be the truth.

V

Thomas, then, did not regard Aristotle primarily as a historical author, any more than he so regarded Augustine or Dionysius Areopagita. He considered them as witnesses for the truth which revealed itself through them, both to himself and, he hoped, to his reader (not only of the *Summa theologica* but also of the commentaries on Aristotle); truth whose validity is established out of itself and by virtue of its own objective arguments. "If the teacher answers a question with mere citations, *nudis auctoritatibus,* then the listener will depart empty-handed, *auditor . . . vacuus abscedet.*"[1] Insofar as philosophizing is in question, a historical author is not of primary interest, even if his name is Aristotle; of primary interest is the truth of the matters at hand.

Thus Thomas examines the texts of Aristotle—which he attempts to illuminate in voluminous commentaries; but he simultaneously examines something beyond the historical Aristotle. And he follows precisely the same procedure with St. Augustine. There is only one text that he treats differently: Holy Scripture, which as the divine Word holds absolute authority for him and is the highest conceivable expression of objective truth. The thing that is sought "beyond" Aristotle and Augustine, as the matter that is really of interest—namely, the truth of the objective world—is precisely what is embodied *in* Holy Scripture. In saying this Thomas by no means contends that it is easy to grasp the meaning of the speech of God as it is made audible in this document of revelation.

Once, when Thomas was attempting to refute a text from Augustine, which he had himself cited as a possible antithesis to his own thinking, he couched his thoughts in a manner memorable both historically and dialectically.[2] He explains his point of view in a single sentence: *ut profundius intentionem Augustini scrutemur et quomodo se habeat veritas circa hoc.* On the one hand, that is, he is unwilling to rest content with the literal sense of the words; he looks behind the text for the author's *intentio,* which is to be grasped at a deeper level. On the other hand, and above all, however, he wants to grasp the truth as his author has formulated it. In this special case, what happens is that Thomas pursues the deeper ramifications of his own opinion, which at first glance seems so far removed from the thesis of Augustine, until it becomes apparent that the differences have lost importance. They are not obliterated, but: *non multum refert,* "it does not matter much" whether one replies as Augustine does or as Thomas himself does.

Dealing with Augustine or Aristotle in this way, concerning oneself with them not primarily as historical authors but as witnesses for the truth—possibly witnesses of genius, but nevertheless not the embodiments of "truth" itself—such dealing "unhistorically" with these writers is simultaneously the truly fruitful way to deal with them so that they affect living history. By such an approach the impulse which motivated Augustine or Aristotle himself, and continued to operate within him, is kept alive —whereas the purely historical approach forever runs the risk of removing the text or author under discussion from the realm of immediacy, from living, intellectual timeliness, and consigning it or him to the realm of the museum, of mere historical interest.

But for Thomas, Aristotle would no longer speak to our intellects, *sine Thoma mutus esset Aristoteles*—this could be said at the beginning of the Modern Age, which was governed more by the historical relationship in itself.[3] The statement is of more timely concern to us at the present moment than may at first appear. Who can say whether we would know anything about Aristotle today, whether we would understand him, whether we would be capable of utilizing his methods of illuminating reality, if it had not been for the special way in which the High Middle Ages received Aristotle, putting primary emphasis upon the truth to be found in him. "The Middle Ages owes an immeasurable debt of gratitude to the Greeks—everyone speaks of that; but the Greeks are likewise indebted to the Middle Ages—and no one speaks of that."[4]

It is not my intention to gloss over the dubious aspects of such unhistorical dealing with historical phenomena. But it would be a great mistake to assume that a man like Thomas was acting out of uncritical, "medieval" naïveté and failed to perceive the special historical quality of Augustine or Aristotle. It was not that; rather, he had taken the position, on firm principle, that this quality was of less importance than the question of truth in what these authors said. In fact, Thomas had a capacity for historical criticism to an extent highly unusual among his contemporaries—that emerges more than once in his work. The *Liber de causis,* so famous in the Middle Ages, was long considered a work of Aristotle's until Thomas, submitting it to literary criticism, discovered that it was in fact a compendium from Proclus.[5] Consider also the mind of a man who in the middle of the thirteenth century could say of the then current astronomical theories: The fact that the phenomena can be explained in this way is no proof of the truth of these theories, for possibly the same phenomena might be explained in a wholly different way, as yet unknown to men: *secundum . . . alium modum nondum ab hominibus comprehensum.*[6] A mind like this can scarcely be called uncritical!

One more brief comment on the subject of "Thomas and Aristotle" is needed. I have said that in accepting Aristotle's outlook on the world Thomas was not appropriating something alien, but recognizing something of his own. This is also true in the sense of a deep temperamental affinity between the two thinkers. This affinity explains something that would otherwise be scarcely understandable: that Thomas had an infallible scent for the real meaning of Aristotle, even when the text before him was unclear or distorted.[7] Thomas himself analyzed this phenomenon, seemingly so modern,[8] in the following manner: There are two basic forms of knowing; on the one hand knowing on the basis of kinship of nature, *per connaturalitatem,* as a man recognizes his beloved or what is his own. The stranger does not understand, or misunderstands, but one who is allied with another in love and congeniality knows immediately, and with absolute certainty, what is meant in a fragment of a letter or a dimly heard call. And on the other hand, says Thomas, there is the *cognoscere per cognitionem,* a knowing of what is alien, an abstract, conceptional, mediate knowing of the mere object.

Nevertheless, in spite of his patent *connaturalitas* with Aristotle, Thomas does not release himself from the obligation to scrutinize the words as they stand with the utmost exactitude and keenness—in this regard differing considerably from Albertus Magnus, who took a far more cavalier attitude toward the text. In fact Albert's confidence in his natural affinity to Aristotle frequently led him to take impermissible liberties in his interpretation. Albert would sometimes claim outright to know what Aristotle would have said about specific questions if he had dealt with them. He went so far as to say: "We will even supplement the missing parts of his incomplete books— whether these are missing because Aristotle did not write them or because they have not come down to us."[9] Thomas would never have allowed himself so rash a statement.

His mind already marked by these two decisions— the entrance into the Dominican Order and his study of Aristotle—Thomas arrived in Paris around 1245, at the age of twenty. At the time he had been compelled to leave Monte Cassino for Naples, he had already come out of seclusion and into the hubbub of a zone of battle: into a city and a university. But Naples had been only a prelude. Paris was not just any city; it was "the capital of Christendom."[10] And the University of Paris, though not the earliest, had long been the most important of the academies of the Western world.

It is, of course, impossible within the framework of these lectures even to sketch the general outlines of the phenomenon comprised within the word "university," or to attempt to tell its history. Nevertheless, certain important points must be recalled.

Point one: The university, in the sense of a corporation, was not a hierarchical institution. The name *universitas* appears for the first time in a papal document of 1208–9.[11] Its significance was at first sociological, though it very soon acquired an "intellectual" meaning. In its sociological sense the word denoted the assemblage, the union, the "guild," the totality, the public, legal body of teachers and students. The second meaning likewise seems to have been in force very early: *universitas litterarum,* totality, comprehensive whole of the sciences, above all of the four faculties of theology, philosophy (*artes*), jurisprudence, and medicine.

The university, then, was not a hierarchical institution.[12] The Church had, it is true, assigned plenipotentiary powers to it. And of course the Pope, through his chancellor, exerted a powerful influence upon it, especially in the case of the University of Paris. (It is wrong to speak of "interference" in this case; in a sense the Pope was simply *chez lui*[13] at the university—in his own house; for the university's autonomy from local and regional political authorities rested upon papal privileges.) Nevertheless, the university was not simply an organ integrated into the hierarchical framework of the Church, like a cathedral chapter or a monastic order.

That was something new in the West, and it was destined to remain something distinctively Occidental, one of the characteristics of Western Christendom. The Christian East, the Eastern Orthodox Church, knows no such phenomenon. In the East it was inconceivable that a corporate body should exist, like the *magistri* of the theological faculty taken as a whole, who possessed firm authority in matters of Christian doctrine (though in a way difficult to comprehend and to describe) without being clearly integrated into the ecclesiastical hierarchy. The situation was pregnant with possibilities of conflict from the start. But the explosive factors were the same as those already inherent in the movement known as "scholasticism"—inherent, in fact, in the Western mind as such, and distinctively characteristic of it.

Incidentally, this authority of *magistri* had existed even before there were any universities in the precise sense of the word. When, for example, King Henry II of England was unable to come to an agreement with Thomas Becket, the Archbishop of Canterbury, he proposed to lay the dispute before the community of Parisian *magistri*. That was in 1169—a generation before the formal establishment of the University of Paris.

Point two: The medieval university was by its nature an institution for the *whole* of Christendom. In practice it was as a rule restricted to the West, but in principle it was open to the entire Christian world. This is a fact highly remarkable in itself, especially in comparison to the present-day university. Whether a man studied or taught at Oxford, Bologna, Paris, Toulouse, Cologne, or Naples, he always remained within the intellectual realm of the Christian West and had no difficulties either of language or of communication. Here was a circumstance whose ramifications were more than merely political or social.

Point three: The medieval university stood in the current of *urban* life. This at first glance purely sociological fact had a great deal to do with its intellectual vitality. Chenu comments: The "Anselm pupils" were transformed into "Abelard pupils."[14] The pupils of Anselm—although they too had asked their prior to write them a theology in which not a single argument would be taken from the Bible—were novices, pupils of the monastic school, living in the seclusion of the Seine valley, provided for by the Abbey of Le Bec, which drew its wealth from landed property. The pupils of Abelard were an entirely different social type. They were the singers of the *carmina burana,* so to speak; they were itinerants moving from one urban university to the next, freely joining together in "nations," terrorizing the citizens of the city and often their professors as well—and so on. The decisive fact about them was their urban stamp, which took the form of a new secularity, an emphatic independence of feudal lords, a new sense of freedom.

From the beginning of the thirteenth century on, all the writings on theology and philosophy no longer came out of abbeys and monastic schools—although, of course, the old monastic orders still existed and now and then produced a masterful piece of work. On the whole, however, scholarly literature henceforth was created in the universities. And when the old monastic orders attempted to raise their studies to the level of the age, they had to leave the cloisters.[15] In the year in which Thomas arrived in Paris, the Abbot of Cîteaux in that city founded a college for his monks, and the Benedictines soon followed his example. ... On the other hand, the early presence of the mendicant friars at the universities is obviously directly connected with the other fact that these young moderns, as associations of preachers, were desirous of living in cities—and incidentally could only live there, for there was not much sense in begging in the wild woods. On the other hand: "It may even be asserted that begging alone afforded them access to the great cities."[16]

To these three characteristics of the medieval university in general—their mediate position between the ecclesiastical hierarchy and free societies; their character as educational institutions for the whole of Western Christendom; their urban stamp—we must add a fourth point which concerns the University of Paris in particular.

As I have said, the University of Paris became the most important university in the West shortly after its establishment around 1200. There are generally a variety of reasons and causes for such a development, not all of which can be traced or even named. But in any case, the University of Paris became the most representative of the medieval universities because, among other things, it was founded in the purest and most radical way upon those branches of knowledge which are "universal" by their own nature: theology and philosophy. No separate branch of knowledge formally poses the question: What is the character of reality as a whole? But theology and philosophy not only cannot dodge this question; they spring directly from it. Thus it is not in the least surprising that the character of the *universitas litterarum* was originally achieved in its pure form neither in Bologna, where jurisprudence was the central subject of studies and teaching, nor in Salerno, where medicine was foremost. Oxford too achieved that character only within limits, for from the beginning empirical science and mathematics dominated there. In the case of Paris, however, we know that the two points around which the life of the university crystallized were theology and philosophy. Curiously enough, they so strongly colored the whole atmosphere of the university that an element which might be considered inseparable from that city seems to have been extinguished—the artistic element. Thus, a kind of student almanac published in 1241 expressly complains that the Muses in Paris have fallen silent.[17]

The University of Paris in the thirteenth century, then, took the lead in philosophical and theological examination of the world, thereby achieving a sort of supremacy. There was, says Denifle, not a single *summa* of the Middle Ages, not a single doctrine of reality that attempted to deal formally with the totality of the universe, which did not derive from Paris.[18] And it was, I think, not a case of mere local patriotism that medieval Paris touted itself as a new Athens. My feeling is that this continuity—from Plato to Thomas Aquinas, let us say—is not an unhistorical construction, and that the notion of the *translatio studii,* the transplantation of the Platonic Academy to the city of the paradigmatic medieval university, is not a mere fiction.[19]

Around 1245, then, twenty-year-old Thomas Aquinas came to the University of Paris, first of all as a learner. Later, as one of its greatest teachers, he would represent in exemplary fashion the universality of this Academy of the Christian West.

VI

The decision in favor of evangelical perfection on the one hand and of Aristotle on the other hand was probably taken by Thomas with utmost deliberation. He no doubt knew very well what he was doing; his decision was the outcome of a single, unitary view of reality. It still remained for him, however, to formulate this view with clarity, to prove the compatibility of the theological and philosophical ways of considering the world. He had to provide good grounds for his fusion of an extremely "theological"—that is, Biblical—theology and an equally extreme "philosophical" philosophy.

But if this was the task Thomas had to set for himself, there was no other place in the entire Western world which offered the young man of twenty more favorable conditions for his own development than the University of Paris. Here the most important teachers were located, the most militant partners in debate, the most radical opposition; here was challenge, creative resistance, and immediate resonance. It is no great exaggeration when Chenu says that Thomas is inconceivable anywhere but at the University of Paris: *Paris est son lieu naturel.*[1]

The truth of the matter is, however, that the University of Paris received very badly indeed its later most celebrated teacher. It refused to admit him to the faculty; it forbade attendance at his inaugural lecture—and so on. It must be added that these difficulties did not really have anything to do with Thomas, with him as an individual or with his intellectual position. Rather, they were an episode in a larger quarrel which has gone down in history under the name of the "Mendicant Controversy."[2] As the name suggests, it had to do with the resistance encountered by the first generations of the mendicant orders, a resistance from within Christendom and in fact from within the ecclesiastical hierarchy. In Paris the disagreement at first took the form of a struggle for teaching chairs, but it gradually developed into a struggle over doctrines—in which a wide spectrum of arguments and motives played their part.

It may virtually be taken for granted that a revolutionary movement which had risen up out of criticism of the existing state of affairs ("things cannot go on this way" more or less sums up the reaction of Dominic to the hopelessly sterile approach of official ecclesiastical circles to the Cathar and Albigensian movement in southern France), a movement which aimed at changing the existing state of affairs, would naturally not be greeted with joy by the powers representative of the existing order. And it might be anticipated that the antagonism would grow all the stronger as the revolutionary movement exerted an ever more potent spell upon the "younger generation"—which, amazingly, is what the mendicant orders did. Finally, in the normal course of events such resistance takes on more strength as the ideal purity of the founders' first impulse vanishes or fades, is overwhelmed and distorted by, for example, fanaticism, or by "professional revolutionaries," or by superficial fellow travelers who are impressed by what is faddishly *outré*.

At any rate, the existing order quite naturally ranged itself strongly against the mendicant orders. As Chesterton put it: We must imagine the shock felt by an aristocratic family whose son entered a mendicant order as rather equivalent to their feelings about an "impossible" marriage ("I have married a gypsy"). Nevertheless, as we know from highly reliable sources, innumerable sons, particularly of noble families, did in fact marry this "gypsy." All the more reason for the existing order in the form of traditional institutions—particularly the ecclesiastical hierarchy of the secular clergy—to oppose such a "disgrace." Their position was well reasoned and by no means a priori contemptible.

We must recall that Dominic, immediately after the formal recognition of his community, dissolved the convent which had been formed at Toulouse and sent his preaching friars out into the world in small groups, literally as beggars. At the same time, to be sure, his goal, which he consistently pursued, was to provide them with a pre-eminently well-founded theological and philosophical education, so that they would be capable of holding their own in the intellectual disputes of the age. He therefore sent his brother monks above all to university cities, and to the universities themselves. The early days of the Dominican Order in Bologna, and in Paris also, were so difficult that at times it seemed as if the plan must die a-borning.

In the case of the Paris group, the Pope himself intervened. He turned not to the bishop but to the university as such, ordering that a church or monastery be placed at the disposal of the Preaching Friars. About a year after the arrival of the first Dominicans, Jean de Barrastre, a professor of theology, turned over to them the hospice of St. Jacques, which he himself had built. The small community of Preaching Friars in Paris formed a sort of student corporation within the university, a legal part of the *universitas magistrorum et scholarium*. Toward the clergy and the citizenry, however, it was a convent, members of whose order lived under a rule and performed choir service; in other words, it was a convent of "regulated canons." Everything seemed to have fallen into place. But there was a tremendous vitality in this small and harmless-seeming group of Preaching Friars, a dynamism that inevitably changed the structure of the entire field of force surrounding them.

They devoted themselves energetically to theological and philosophical studies; but their chief desire was to operate publicly—as pastors, as preachers, as teachers. And they wanted to do so outside the framework of the regular ecclesiastical administration. In concrete terms that meant independently of the parish organization. This independence had, to be sure, been guaranteed them by the Pope. From the time of their founding the mendicant orders were "exempt," that is, they were removed by papal decree from the jurisdiction of the regular local authorities and placed directly under the authority of the papacy. Such a special set-up, however, is by nature a two-edged proposition; Bernard of Clairvaux had long ago violently attacked it as an institution.[3] On the one hand, here was an instrument by which the supreme authority of the Church could put across reforms important for the whole of the Church

—against the resistance of the institutionalized bureaucracy, against the natural sluggishness of such an apparatus, and over its head. On the other hand, to grant such exemption could not help but unsettle the stability of the normal routine. What was more, the central authority was far away and the exemptees were therefore usually "out of range," so that in practice they could do or not do pretty much as they pleased.

Once legally established, then, the Preaching Friars, like the Franciscans, forced their way into public ministries with enormous dynamism; that was what they had been founded for, after all. But no one could have predicted the speed with which these communities would grow in numbers and intellectual importance. In September 1217 the first Dominicans arrived in Paris—barely a year after the official founding of the order. Again barely a year later, in August 1218, St. Jacques was founded. The following spring, Dominic, making a visitation, found a community that already consisted of thirty monks. Five years later their number had quadrupled. And the new members were all masters and scholars of the university. Nor did the Dominican community in Paris grow only numerically; it also became an intellectual center. People flocked to Dominican sermons. We learn, from a polemic written by Thomas, one of the points which was apparently raised against the Dominicans' work of preaching the faith. This new type of preaching, the argument ran, exposed the bishops to the contempt of the people because the bishops did not preach that way: *ergo talis praedicatio religiosorum periculosa est Ecclesiae Dei,* "therefore such preaching by the mendicant friars is a danger to the Church of God."[4] To which Thomas replies: No one should be hindered from doing something well just because others will be held in contempt because of him; rather, those who make themselves worthy of contempt should be hindered.[5] These are unusually harsh words. The struggle between the secular clergy and the mendicant friars was in full swing.

The deepest reason for the secular clergy's enmity—so said Bonaventura, the Franciscan[6]—was the fact that the mendicant orders absorbed some income of the secular clergy. This is not necessarily equated with avarice. We know that the income of the lower parish clergy during the Middle Ages was "literally wretched."[7] They were fighting for sheer existence in the economic sense. And I wonder whether we ought not to find this quite understandable; I wonder whether we may say simply that the secular clergy "opposed a necessary reform of pastoral care out of fear for its income." Scheeben[8] ascribes this motive to the parish clergy of St. Benoit and of the cathedral chapter of Notre Dame, in whose district the Monastery of St. Jacques was situated.

To be sure, the details add up to a rather dismal and pettifogging picture; for example, the parishioners of St. Benoit were ordered to attend their own parish church on five specified high holidays—that is, *not* to go to the Dominicans. And the Dominicans were compelled, under threat of excommunication, to make public announcements of this ordinance. If any offerings were nevertheless made in the Dominican church on those holidays, the sums had to be turned over to the parish church. The Preaching Friars were permitted to ring only one bell, and this bell must weigh no more than three hundred pounds. It could be rung only to call the friars to prayers. If a member of the parish wanted to be buried with the Dominicans, the funeral mass must be held in the parish church. And so forth and so on.[9] A tremendous campaign of slander was waged; word was spread that the mendicant friars were guilty of a variety of misdeeds not susceptible to definite proof—above all legacy-hunting. In this way the emotions of the rabble were roused. By the time Thomas came to Paris, things had reached such a pitch that the Preaching Friars scarcely dared to venture out on the street for fear of insults and physical attack. King Louis IX—St. Louis—found it necessary to have royal troops guard the Monastery of St. Jacques.

Here, too, of course, right and wrong, sanctity and profanity, were divided between both parties. In regard to "violence," for example—we know that the Dominican scholars on occasion assaulted the rector of the university, who was a member of the secular clergy. And the superiors of the mendicant orders had repeatedly to remind the friars to display respect for the *praelati Ecclesiae*.[10] The Master General of the Dominicans, Humbert of Romans, gives some droll examples of provocatory behavior in one of his circular letters. For example, the friars should not set for their preaching the very same hour at which the bishop usually gave his sermons. And although Bonaventura said, as I have already mentioned, that the secular clergy's chief bone of contention was the question of money, he also said of his own brothers in the order: sometimes money was "avariciously begged for, recklessly accepted, and even more recklessly consumed."[11]

The mendicant orders, then, faced ill will everywhere, but in Paris the feeling was all the stronger when the new faction began to conquer the university. The battle that flared up over this was an extremely involved affair. On the one hand, all the ordinary elements of conflict between the secular clergy and the mendicant monks were increased and intensified by the rivalry for teaching chairs. On the other hand, a wholly new element also entered in. The enmity of the university to the mendicant friars began to be aimed at the Pope—or we may also say, at the chancellor, who was the Pope's executive organ within the university. Papal privilege had originally founded and guaranteed the freedom of the university—freedom, that is, from the supervision of local political and ecclesiastical rule and rulers. This, too, was a kind of exemption. But then the guarantor of that freedom, the chancellor appointed by the Pope, became a danger to freedom, to the freedom of organization and self-determination held by the *universitas magistrorum*.

This body of teachers very soon came to regard itself as privileged, one might almost say, as a kind of "trade union"—against the chancellor. The chancellor, as representative of the Pope, had far-reaching powers. He was the magistrate who in special cases might even pronounce excommunication. Above all, he issued the permit to teach, the *licentia docendi*. The individual master was in practice wholly defenseless against the chancellor's decisions. But of course the collectivity of teachers, the *universitas* as such, could throw considerable weight into the balance—provided that it was capable of concerted action as a *universitas* and had an advocate who could gain the ear of the Pope. This last was soon accomplished; the appointment of an advocate at the papal Curia was moved and approved between 1215 and 1220.[12] But of course this was not enough to safeguard the interests of the *universitas,* as was to become apparent when the mendicant friars began applying for teaching chairs.

The very first Dominican professor in Paris, Roland of Cremona, had been called to his chair by a curious set of circumstances—brought in, we may almost say, as a "strikebreaker." The *universitas magistrorum et scholarium,* the professors and students, had actually gone "on strike." They had even left the city of Paris, in protest against the civil guard's killing of one student and injuring of several others in the course of riots and brawls at carnival time. The Dominicans, naturally, were not affected; they remained in Paris in their Monastery of St. Jacques, which again seems perfectly natural. And at this very time, in the year 1229, they acquired their first teaching chair. Two years later a professor belonging to the secular clergy asked to be admitted to the Dominican Order. Thus another academic chair devolved upon the Dominicans, who, of course, were determined not to let this second chair which had come their way slip out of their hands again. During the same period the Franciscans captured their first teaching chair in a similar manner: one of the leading professors of theology entered the community of the *fratres minores* at the age of nearly sixty. He was Alexander of Hales, the teacher of Bonaventura.

And now, in the year 1252, the Dominicans fetched Thomas Aquinas, now twenty-seven, the "assistant" of Albertus Magnus, from Cologne to give lectures in Paris on Peter Lombard's *Book of Sentences*. These lectures were to be held at the order's academy in the Monastery of St. Jacques. This was not the same thing, to be sure, as at the university, but it was the first step toward it. The chancellor welcomed such activities; after all, these men, Alexander of Hales, Albert, Bonaventura, and Thomas, were the finest minds of the time. It was simply a fact that the avant-garde intelligentsia were gathering in the mendicant orders. Van Steenberghen remarks in his comprehensive survey of the situation at the universities between 1250 and 1275 that at this time, both in Paris and in Oxford, there was not a single theologian of the secular clergy who deserves mention.[13] When the Cistercians wished to establish the study of theology in their home monastery of Cîteaux, they had to ask for a magister from the Order of Preachers.[14] Hence it cannot very well be said that the chancellor was acting against the interests of the University of Paris (though he may have enjoyed the sensation of exercising power) when he so readily issued the *licentia docendi* to applicants from the mendicant orders, for example to Bonaventura and to Thomas Aquinas—who received his *licentia* in 1256. Yet this act was the straw that broke the camel's back. The *universitas magistrorum,* that association of professors based on voluntary membership, refused to accept either Bonaventura or Thomas. And so these outsiders were barred from membership in the *universitas magistrorum.*

In 1252—the year that Thomas came from Cologne to Paris—the *magistri* of the secular clergy had already held a meeting which was kept secret from the chancellor and the professors of the monastic orders.[15] Among the decisions of this meeting was the following: only one professor from each order should be accepted into the faculty of the university. This, curiously, was justified by a pious citation from the New Testament: *nolite plures magistri fieri* (James iii. 1)—which certainly does *not* mean: do not desire to become several *magistri.* Furthermore, the students were to be forbidden to attend the lectures of those whom the *magistri* had not accepted as members of the faculty, that is, those whose sole accreditation was the chancellor's *licentia.* Those received into the faculty must subscribe to this rule under oath.

These new regulations were applied when Thomas received the *licentia docendi* from the chancellor. The faculty forbade the students to attend his lectures. The Pope now insisted that the two mendicant friars be accepted— whereupon the corporate body of the *magistri,* which was after all a voluntary organization, countered by simply dissolving itself. The Pope refused to permit such mutinies; he issued a special breve, in which Thomas and Bonaventura were mentioned by name, ordering that the pair be allowed to teach publicly. This was done in 1257.

For Bonaventura the new regulation came too late; at the age of thirty-six he had been called to the office of supreme head of the entire Franciscan Order, and had thus cut short his career as scholar and professor. For Thomas, too, of course, that formal edict did not settle everything; in 1259, while he was preaching, someone stood up and in a loud voice read a verse lampoon against the mendicant friars. That someone was a partisan of Professor William of St. Amour, a member of the Parisian secular clergy who had already been sent into exile by Louis IX, but whose polemic against the mendicant orders continued to exercise considerable sway (it was even translated into the vulgar tongue and its arguments crop up in secular literature, for example in the *Roman de la Rose*).

William of St. Amour's polemic was written on commission from the university and with the encouragement of the French episcopate. Its title was *De periculis novissimorum temporum,* On the Dangers of the Last Times.[16] It was a witty pamphlet in which the author brought up all the objections which the official Church had itself raised against the voluntary poverty movement one and two generations before.[17] As one of its principal points it contested the claim of the mendicant orders that they exemplified a way of life according to the Gospel. He who does not work shall not eat; he who wishes to give up everything for Christ's sake ought to work or enter a monastery, but he ought not to beg; never was it reported that Christ or the Apostles begged; the "good shepherd" does not beg from his flock—and so on. As we see, these were attacks based very much on principle, and were not easy to parry. But the most dangerous aspect of this pamphlet was its conclusion: that something must be done against these pseudo-apostles whose appearance signalized the coming of the Last Days. The *novissima tempora* were intended eschatologically, and the pamphlet played upon all the age's anxieties concerning the Last Days. Steps had to be taken against this sinister crew. William of St. Amour formulated, in a highly suggestive manner, a few terse imperatives. The dangerous ones must be isolated; their followers must be weaned from them; new followers must be prevented from coming to them. Above all, they must be forbidden to preach and teach.

In the midst of the fierce dispute raging around him, Thomas had already written the first books of his *Commentary on the Sentences* and tried his wings at philosophy in *De ente et essentia*. Now he drafted his first polemic, against William of St. Amour: *Contra impugnantes Dei cultum et religionem* (*religio* here means "religious order"). Two other polemics were to follow this first defense of the life of evangelical perfection.

In a public disputation—it was more or less a forum open to all—a cunning question was put to Thomas: Should not a member of a religious order, who had after all chosen to walk the way of perfection, simply suffer the attacks of enemies without offering any defense? To this Thomas replied: Yes, insofar as his own person is concerned; the member of an order must even be prepared to endure far worse than hostile words.[18] But where the attack is leveled against the evangelical way of life itself, which is to say, against divine teachings, the answer must be no.

This distinction governed the tone of these polemics. They show no trace of personal feeling; in fact, they are "polemical" only in the formal sense, for they are not really disputatious. Nevertheless, strong personal conviction can be felt in the freshness and vigor of the diction.

In one of these essays Thomas cites the following objection: Is it not improbable that the way of life founded by Christ, the way of spiritual perfection, should have slumbered from the age of the Apostles right down to the very

74

founding of the mendicant orders?[19] His answer is: Of course it did not slumber—but are not different things needful in different times? And there follows a statement exemplifying the whole intellectual intensity of the era (this last polemic appeared in the year 1270, the time of Thomas' second period of teaching in Paris and the time of his greatest fecundity and strongest influence). The statement is:

"What then shall we reply if someone should ask: Has Christian doctrine slumbered since the times of the great masters Athanasius, Basil, Ambrose, Augustine, and their contemporaries—slumbered down to these times in which men are again concerning themselves in greater measure with Christian doctrine? Shall it then be impermissible, as that strange doctrine holds, to take up again something good which for a time has been neglected? If that were so, then it would be impermissible for anyone to take martyrdom upon himself. . . ."[20]

We cannot here discuss in detail the content of these polemical essays. We must, however, speak of the spirit in which Thomas conducted this discussion. It was the spirit of the disciplined debate, a form of argumentation which, for all its clear militancy, remains a dialogue. We may also say: it was the spirit of the *disputatio*. In saying this, we touch upon the subject of the next lecture.

VII

There is no evidence that St. Thomas participated in the rivalries of university politics during his stay in Paris. From all we know of Thomas, it is highly improbable that he entered this arena at all. But he did intervene in the *doctrinal* disputes over the realization of *perfectio evangelica,* and contributed several essays on the subject. These writings are definitely polemics—and, moreover, not the only works of this type that Thomas produced; during the last five years of his life he wrote several others, directed against an opponent with whom everyone is wont to confuse him. But we shall have more to say of this matter later.

The diction of these essays is, as might be expected, more spontaneous, more vigorous, and of course more contentious than we usually find in the works of Thomas. "This argument rather deserves to be laughed at than to be answered"—*magis derisione quam responsione dignum est*[1]—that is not Thomas' usual language. Or: "If anyone wants to contest this, let him not babble about the matter in front of boys, but let him rather publicly present a pamphlet on it, so that those who have insight will be able to judge what is true and to refute what is false with the authority of truth."[2] His late polemic, *De unitate intellectus,* closes on a similar note: "If anyone who boastfully claims the deceptive name of science for himself has anything to say against what we have written here, let him not do so in privacy and before boys, who have no judgment on such difficult matters, but let him himself write against this work, if he dares. . . ."[3] And so forth.

The tone is belligerent, certainly. However, these works have another characteristic far more important and also far more typical of Thomas. We have already spoken of the possibility that an unsuspecting reader, rather stunned and confused, may read whole pages containing nothing but opposing arguments formulated in a highly convincing manner. There will be nothing at all in the phraseology to indicate that Thomas rejects these arguments—not the trace of a hint at the weakness of the argument, not the slightest nuance of ironical exaggeration. The opponent himself speaks, and an opponent who is obviously in splendid form, calm, objective, moderate. I may read, for example, in Thomas' first polemic, written at the age of thirty: He who accepts a gift becomes dependent upon the giver. Members of a religious order, however, ought properly be free of all worldly dependence, since they are called to freedom of the spirit. . . . Hence they may not live on alms.[4] Or: Members of an order profess the estate of perfection. According to the New Testament (Acts xx. 35), however, it is more perfect to give alms than to receive them. Therefore they ought to work in order to possess something which they can then share with the needy, rather than to receive and live by alms.[5] Or: He who lives at the table of others necessarily becomes a flatterer.[6] Or: The Apostle Paul refused to accept money for his support from the Corinthians, in order not to supply a pretext [for defamation] to the apostles of lies.[7] And so on. All these arguments sound—*nota bene,* in the formulation given them by St. Thomas himself—very plausible and reasonable. Polemic as we know it has not prepared us for this sort of thing. We are so little prepared for it that frequently the opposing arguments have been ascribed to St. Thomas himself, because he expounds them so convincingly and apparently (in appearance only!) is convinced by them.[8]

We have already said that Thomas succeeds not only in presenting the opponent's divergent or flatly opposed opinion, together with the underlying line of reasoning, but also, many times, in presenting it better, more clearly, and more convincingly than the opponent himself might be able to do. In this procedure there emerges an element profoundly characteristic of St. Thomas' intellectual style: the spirit of the *disputatio,* of disciplined opposition; the spirit of genuine discussion which remains a dialogue even while it is a dispute. This spirit governs the inner structure of all St. Thomas' works. And I feel that in this generosity of spirit, too, the exemplary, the paradigmatic character of the *doctor communis* of Christendom is displayed.

Let us give a few moments' thought to dialogue and the part it plays in mankind's community life. Such conversation has as its aim not only communication, but also the clarifying of ideas, the finding and illuminating of truth—for both parties to the conversation, of course, do not hold the same opinions from the start. Plato, it would appear, went so far as to assert that truth emerges as a human reality in conversation *alone:* "By conversing many times, and by long, familiar intercourse for the matter's sake, a light is kindled in a flash, as by a flying spark. . . ."[9] In fact, Plato calls even solitary thinking and cognition "a soundless conversation of the soul within itself."[10] Socrates, who represents for Plato *the* prototypal seeker after truth and finder of knowledge, was forever engaged in conversation and in testing himself and his interlocutor in debate.

Augustine, as a Platonist, introduced this fundamental attitude into his discussions with theological adversaries. But even Aristotle, whose style of thinking at first sight seems to lean less toward dialogue than toward thesis and system, remarks that if one wishes to find the truth one must first consider the opinions of those who judge differently;[11] and he speaks of the joint labor of disputation where it is of prime importance to be a good companion and collaborator. This remark is to be found in Aristotle's *Topics,*[12] in that section of the organon which came to the knowledge of the schools of the West during the twelfth century, as a kind of second installment; it went by the name of *Logica nova* and was instantly understood and seized upon as an aid to the systematic development of the art of disputation.[13] "Without the Eighth Book of the

Topics," says the secular, cosmopolitan writer John of Salisbury, "people dispute at hazard, but not with artistic understanding"—*non disputatur arte, sed casu.*[14]

It was in the twelfth century, then, that the rules of the game of debate were artistically formulated and developed. "To every *disputatio legitima* there belong question, answer, thesis, agreement, negation, argument, proof, and concluding formulation of the result"—thus states a certain Magister Radulfus.[15] During the last decades of the twelfth century disputation was well entrenched in the academies of the West. In fact, it became more or less obligatory; it dominated the whole scene of higher educational activity. Concurrently, to be sure, degeneration and abuse set in, so that thoughtful men began to complain about hairsplitting and logomachy, about purely formalistic wrangling.[16] "This intellectual gymnastics for display and for amusement"—so it was described by Hegel[17] who somewhat unfairly applied the term to medieval scholasticism in general (for which reason it was unjust and inaccurate). Apparently there was no preventing such perversions. We find evidence for the same sort of thing in the Platonic dialogue: Socrates makes a strong plea to Gorgias, his interlocutor, not to make any "speeches" but to accept the conversational mode. Whereupon his opponent snaps back: "You will see that nobody surpasses me in this art of short answers; that too is one of the arts I can boast of."[18] Which means that the form which Socrates has proposed solely in order to avoid the formalistic trifling of sophistic verbal trickery becomes, in a trice, another variety of formalistic trifling.

When Thomas, around the middle of the thirteenth century, took up the already well-developed instrument of the scholastic *disputatio* in order to play his own melody upon it, the first thing he had to do was to change it: to omit, to simplify, to prune. The preface to the *Summa theologica* speaks of the "excessive accumulation of needless questions, articles, and arguments"; and Thomas, as Grabmann observes, vigorously sweeps under the table a vast number of the by then customary schoolmasterly over-subtleties.[19] (Late scholasticism was to pull them out again and display them in all their splendor, *on* the table!)

But for Thomas, too, as we have said, the framework of the disputation governs the form of his entire written work. The *articulus,* which forms the smallest building block of the *Summa theologica* as well as of the *Quaestiones disputatae* and the *Quaestiones quodlibetales*—the *articulus* first formulates the question at issue. It then adduces, not the opinions of the author himself, but rather the voices of the opposition. Only after this does the author himself take the floor, first offering a systematically developed answer to the question and then replying to each of the opposing arguments.

In this manner, for example, the subject of "passion and moral action" is posed for discussion in the *Summa theologica.*[20] The question is asked whether the degree of passion of an action increases or diminishes the moral value of this action. And the first argument declares that passion clouds rational judgment; hence it diminishes the moral value of the action. The second argument: God and pure spirits know no passion; therefore passionlessness adds to moral value. Third argument: to do wrong out of passion is obviously less bad than to do wrong with clear premeditation; conversely, to do a good action through passion subtracts from the value of the action—and so on. As yet Thomas himself has not spoken; he himself first takes the floor in the *corpus* of the article, which develops the question from the very bottom, and answers it. In this case his answer runs: that "to act *out* of passion" diminishes both the value and the unworthiness of an action; that on the other hand, "to act *with* passion" increases both, the value and the unworthiness also.[21] And then Thomas proceeds to answer the arguments formulated at the beginning.

It may be that we are alienated by such a mode of presentation. I should like to propose that we examine this alienation a little more closely. What exactly is it that puts us off? I think that it is first of all the schematization, the formalism, the stereotyped nature of the presentation. And secondly, it is the fact that the content of the arguments advanced does not affect us, that they are not *our* arguments. Both these elements, however, have little to do with the core of the matter. The core is that we are dealing with a dialogue. At bottom the scholastic *articulus* is quite close to the Platonic dialogue. And if we would think of the scholastic *articulus* brushed clean of the dust of the past, we would find it, I think, an exciting affair. Let us take a contemporary problem that concerns us and formulate it as a question. Then, in the most precise and concise language, the difficulties are presented—the real, weighty counter-arguments. Then comes a clear, ordered exposition of the answer. Finally, on the basis of this systematically developed answer, there follows an exact reply to the counter-arguments. And all this is compressed into one or two printed pages—that being the typical length of a scholastic *articulus* of the great period. "No writers have ever said more with a stricter economy of words," says Gilson.[22] It would be difficult to conceive of any livelier form—and any that makes greater intellectual demands upon the writer!

Thomas, moreover, did not only *write* in this form. In his own teaching at the University of Paris he cultivated the oral *disputatio* to an extent hitherto unknown.[23] In fact, Thomas actually appears to have invented a particular form, the *disputatio de quolibet,* the "free" discussion whose subject in each case is directly suggested by the audience.[24] And he poured tremendous energy into this mode of teaching; probably it was also an enormous pleasure to him. We know that during the three years from 1256 to 1259 Thomas regularly held two major disputations a week. Each of the extended articles of the *Quaestiones disputatae*—there are more than five hundred of them!—is the fruit of a public disputation.

The decisive factor, of course, is the spirit that dominated and informed these discussions—which, naturally, was not synonymous with the external form (as, on the other hand, there can be forms without the spirit). What can be said, then, about the ethos of the debate?

The first point is this: Anyone who considers dialogue, disputation, debate, to be a fundamental method for arriving at truth must already have concluded and stated that arriving at truth is an affair that calls for more power than the autarchic individual possesses. He must feel that common effort, perhaps the effort of everybody, is necessary. No one is sufficient unto himself and no one is completely superfluous; each person needs the other; the teacher even needs the student, as Socrates always held. In any case, the learner, the student, contributes something to the dialogue along with the teacher.

If this fundamental conviction is genuine, it must necessarily affect the mode of listening as well as the mode of speaking. Dialogue does not mean only that people talk to one another, but also that they listen to one another. The first requirement, therefore, is: Listen to the interlocutor, take note of his argument, his contribution to the *recherche collective de la vérité,* in the same way that he himself understands his own argument.[25] There was one rule of the *disputatio legitima* which made this kind of listening mandatory: No one was permitted to answer directly to the interlocutor's objection; rather, he must first repeat the opposing objection in his own words, thus explicitly making sure that he fully understood what his opponent had in mind. Let us for a moment imagine that the same rule were put into effect again nowadays, with infraction of it resulting in automatic disqualification. How this would clear the air in public debate! Incidentally, Socrates had followed this practice, long ago, even if he had not formulated it as a rule. In the dialogue on immortality in the *Phaedo* Socrates first reviews the objections which his friends have reluctantly made. And then he asks: "Is it this, Simmias and Cebes, which we have to examine? They both agreed that these were the questions." And later he adds that he is stating Cebes' objection "again and again on purpose, that nothing may escape us."[26]

This remark reveals the primary function of such listening. Socrates is not on the alert to catch his opponent's "weak spots," not concerned from the very beginning with how he is going to refute his opponent's arguments, but is primarily aiming at a deeper grasp of the substance. This is not principally a question of "decency," and certainly not of some vague "modesty" (which was simply unknown in either classical or Christian ethics); it is a question of, precisely, what Paul Valéry once formulated as follows: "The first thing to be done by a person who wishes to refute an opinion is this: he must make it his own somewhat better than the person who best defends it."[27] We listen in order to become fully aware of the real strength of the opposing argument. Thomas seems actually to assume that we ourselves cannot recognize or anticipate the possible objections to a thesis. The concrete elements of a situation which might put a new face upon the matter cannot be predetermined. In every serious utterance by an opponent some one of the many facets of reality is expressed. There is always something right and truthful in his words; and although this something may be minimal, the refutation must begin there if it is to be convincing. It is with this idea in mind, I think, that Thomas—in the *Summa Against the Pagans*—regrets that the statements of the *mahumetistae et pagani* are not available to him in detail, "so that from what they say we might be able to extract reasons to destroy their error."[28]

But of course this listening is not concerned solely with grasping the substance. It is also directed fully at the interlocutor as a person; it draws its vitality from respect for the other's dignity, and even from gratitude toward him— gratitude for the increase in knowledge which is derived even from error. "We must love them both, those whose opinions we share and those whose opinions we reject. For both have labored in the search for truth and both have helped us in the finding of it."[29]

The great doctors of Christendom completely agree on this point; they stand in a common front against the stupidity of narrow-minded polemic. For the latter usually lacks not only respect for the person of the opponent but also full openheartedness to the truth of things. The attitude formulated by Thomas—which has nothing in common with sentimentality—is in keeping with the best, the most legitimate tradition.

Here, for example, is an extract from an essay of St. Augustine *against* the Manichaeans: "Let those rage against you who do not know with what toil truth is found . . .; let those rage against you who do not know with what difficulty the inner man's eye becomes sound; . . . let those rage against you who do not know how many groans and sighs accompany the winning of even a tiny morsel of divine insight."[30] And when John Henry Newman in his *Grammar of Assent* engages in polemic against John Locke, he takes this tone: "I have so great a respect both for the character and the ability of Locke, for his manly simplicity of mind and his outspoken candour . . . that I feel no pleasure in considering him in the light of an opponent to views which I myself have ever cherished as true."[31]

That is the spirit of genuine disputation, and Thomas also embodies it. A contemporary remarks that Thomas would refute his opponents as one teaches a pupil.[32]

In line with this, we must call attention to one more magnificent statement from the *Summa Against the Pagans*. Thomas has just set forth the ideas of Averroës and Aristotle on man's ultimate felicity; he has shown how in spite of a correct starting point they could not help missing the essential. At this point he says, with sovereign charity: *in quo satis apparet, quantam angustiam patiebantur hinc inde eorum praeclara ingenia*[33]—in which is revealed how much these illustrious minds must have suffered from such confinement.

Disputatio, however, involves not only listening to another, but also addressing oneself to him. The interlocutor in a disputation declares, by his very participation, his willingness to take a position and answer for it. He lays himself open to correction.

First of all, of course, in order for the whole process to take place meaningfully, he lets himself be heard. That is not by any means a matter to be taken for granted—namely, that he should speak in such a way that the other can hear him, that is, that the other can take in his argument as clearly and completely as possible. When a person speaks in the spirit of genuine *disputatio,* his primary wish is to clarify the substance. Hence he must make a point of speaking comprehensively (which, naturally, does not mean reducing his subject to simplistic terms. Arbitrary, eccentric, and esoteric jargon is contrary to the spirit of genuine debate.

To be sure, debate—and perhaps every conversation—implies several voices, polyphony; every voice strikes its own note—but not simply for the sake of airing itself, any more than proper listening is undertaken out of some misty form of modesty. Just as we listen so that the interlocutor may have the chance to express himself in his own voice, so we express ourselves when our turn comes—and likewise for the sake of illuminating the substance, of which we may have caught some glimpse which has eluded our adversary. Only through this does there take place that mutual opposition, which according to Thomas is the very best way to reveal the truth:[34] "Iron sharpens iron" (Prov. xxvii. 17). There is no trace in all this of mere sentimental deference to "what the other fellow thinks." Rather, this technique has as its sole purpose the clarification of the objective substance. Clarification always means that something is made clear *to someone.* This someone is the adversary. Clarifying speech in particular is animated by respect for the adversary. He is respected as a fellow seeker after truth. Disputing, conducting genuine debate, means expressly granting the other the right both to understand what we mean and critically to examine our statements for their truth or falsehood.

As soon as we state this definition, we realize that the principle is by no means as self-evident as it may seem. Among Ernst Jünger's aphorisms is the sentence: "He who provides a commentary on himself is stooping beneath his level."[35] A very fine-sounding epigram. But what is Jünger actually saying? Suppose he has written or said something that we feel we do not understand and may have to challenge. We therefore say: What do you mean by that obscure statement; is it really true, and how does it accord with other propositions which appear to be unassailably right? But he will not deign to answer us. Instead, he recommends a portentous silence. We all know how common such portentous silences are. But the really great teachers of the Western world—from Socrates and Augustine (who spoke on the highest truths to the fishermen of Hippo) to Thomas and Kant (in whose *Critique of Pure Reason* we may read: "To be refuted . . . is no danger, but not to be understood is one"[36])—all these great teachers are marked by a magnificent inner security. They are not afraid of lowering themselves or diminishing their superiority by the use of simple language. They are perfectly able to manipulate solemn and sometimes highly emotional phraseology; but they never think themselves too important and they never hesitate for a moment to "stoop beneath their level," if by so doing they can speak the truth more clearly, clarify the matter for "someone else," for the interlocutor, the pupils, the person in error. In true disputation this other person is neither ignored by the speaker, nor bluffed, nor merely "worked over," spellbound, misled or, to put it crudely, "done in." Men who want not so much to clarify as to create a sensation are unfitted for debate—and they will avoid it. That point was, as a matter of fact, made as early as the twelfth century in defense of the *disputatio*. The disputation, it was held, was an excellent means of unmasking empty noise, oratory, "belletristics," and rhetoric, of keeping such devices from obstructing the search for truth and of repressing those who were not interested in the *scire* but in the *sciri*, not in knowing but in being known.[37]

There are numerous tokens by which Thomas considered the spirit of the *disputatio* equivalent to the spirit of the university itself. In the medieval university it was no

87

more possible than it is today to achieve universality of knowledge and present things in such a way that students, or even teachers, obtained a truly "integral view." In this sense the medieval university, just like our own universities, was not a place for *studium generale*. But there was a difference: the medieval university had the *disputatio,* and through it universality was achieved! Hence we may validly ask whether the disappearance of disciplined debate carried out within the framework of the university between individuals and among the faculties may not be the true reason for the much-lamented loss of even a sketchy integral view. It should be clear that I am not speaking here of converse among specialists and on a subject interesting only to specialists. I mean converse on the subjects of "man in general." On these subjects, of course, the separate disciplines are constantly raising new questions and offering new material for discussion. I know that for a debate of this nature several prerequisites are needed which were obviously present in the medieval university and which seem lacking today—for example, the common language and the relatively unitary philosophical and theological world view. But perhaps it would not be altogether utopian to attempt to rebuild our academies on the basis of those very principles which were the foundation stones of the Occidental university—one of which is certainly the spirit of disputation.

I have already mentioned the clearing of the public mind which might result from an allegiance to the specific rules of disputation. Naturally, one can only postulate such a thing in *modus irrealis*. But if anyone should ask how public discussion could have so hopelessly degenerated, perhaps the answer may be that only the paradigm has been lacking, only the "model," the commanding example of the *disputatio* in the very place where it naturally ought to be at home: the university.

From the moment that Thomas was officially accepted into the faculty of the University of Paris in 1257, he set himself to his ultimate task, which he was never thereafter to abandon. In spite of the variety of assignments that were heaped upon him, and in spite of the moving around he had to do, at bottom he remained all along and wherever he was, one thing above all: a teacher. As a sideline he also organized a number of faculties, founded schools, drew up and approved curricula. At the chapter-general of the Dominican Order, held in Valenciennes in 1259, Thomas—then a young professor—joined his former master Albertus Magnus on a commission which established a new code on studies for the entire order; among other points it stipulated that every province of the order must create a school of the *artes liberales,* with *philosophie en tête.*[1] Nevertheless, Thomas was not really an administrator, but a teacher, and he remained that until the end.

Because of their singularity we shall speak briefly of two assignments which came to Thomas from outside the Dominican Order, and which he took on in addition to his other duties. The first of these concerned the separation of the Eastern Church from Rome. The final break had come in the eleventh century, and thus the separation had lasted for almost two hundred years. The new Eastern Roman Emperor, Michael Palaeologus, desired re-unification. Although the Emperor was motivated chiefly by political reasons, Pope Urban IV, who had formerly been Patriarch of Jerusalem, responded to the Emperor's overtures. Naturally, however, he insisted upon the resolving of doctrinal differences.

This seemed virtually impossible—all the more so since foolish polemics had long since so completely beclouded the common elements of belief that these had almost dropped out of sight. Here was a situation where an extraordinary arbiter was needed, an unimpassioned, unpolemical, sincere mind concerned only for the truth, capable of impartial judgment of disputed points. And this was the role that Urban IV assigned to St. Thomas. He was given an anti-Greek polemic with the request that he analyze it carefully and pick out the real points of controversy.

The task rather exceeded Thomas' powers (for one thing, Thomas had only an extremely inadequate knowledge of the Greek language; for another thing, the polemic relied heavily upon forged documents which simply could not be detected with the resources of textual criticism available to the thirteenth century—and so on). Nevertheless, St. Thomas' small essay *Against the Errors of the Greeks* (1263) is important for several reasons. In it, for instance, he formulates and advocates the principle of "benevolent interpretation," that is to say, an interpretation which endeavors, as far as possible, to regard the text in question as understandable and acceptable. He also expounds the impossibility of intelligibly translating an idea from one language to another by translating "word for word." In spite of his inadequate knowledge of Greek it appears that Thomas had learned by personal experience that translation, strictly speaking, is something altogether impossible; that the many-faceted idea is expressed differently, and yet equally rightly and truly, in each language after its own fashion. It is no wonder, *non est mirum,* as Thomas says in the preface, and is to be expected, that discordances will arise if translation is done *quod verbum sumatur ex verbo,* by using the synonymous Latin word for each Greek word.[2] Rather, the wording must be altered if the sense is really to be carried over into the other language.

In spite of the unavoidable inadequacies of this treatise, reunion of the Greek and Roman Churches actually took place at the time, although the compact did not last long; at the Council of Lyons in 1274 the union was solemnly sworn, after the Gospel had been sung in Latin and Greek at a festive divine service.[3] Albertus Magnus was there, Bonaventura was also present, and Thomas had been invited—but he died on the way to Lyons.

Around the same time (1263) this same Pope Urban IV commissioned Thomas to compose or collate the texts for the liturgical celebration of Corpus Christi day, which was inaugurated during his papacy. There were to be readings, prayers, antiphons, hymns, and sequences. Thomas undertook the task, and what he produced is certainly unusual. It is hard to believe that this is the work of the author of the sober *Quaestiones disputatae* and the *Summa theologica.* The authorship of the poems may not be entirely his—this is true of many thirteenth-century poems—but it is amazing to hear Thomas saying: *Lauda, Sion, salvatorem, Lauda ducem et pastorem, In hymnis et canticis.*

There is another aspect to this matter, however, and one which relates to Aquinas the theologian rather than Aquinas the philosopher. I should like to dwell upon it a moment. It is often said, and rightly, that the Middle Ages were a time in which an increasingly "subjective" piety drifted further and further away from the major "objective" forms of the ritual mystery, especially from the public sacrifice as the center of the ritual and the religion; and that such subjective forms of worship even penetrated into the sphere of ritual proper. The introduction of the Corpus Christi celebration has been taken, with some justification, as a step along this path, and insofar

91

as Thomas played a major part in this innovation, he has been regarded as the foremost figure who helped to found and virtually "introduced" those forms of Eucharistic piety separate from the celebration of the public sacrifice.

However, anyone who reads the treatise on the Eucharist in the *Summa theologica* will be surprised to find exactly the opposite thesis enunciated there. For Thomas says that the celebration of the sacrifice is *the* place for the sacrament; "this sacrament is *simultaneously* sacrifice and sacrament."[4] Furthermore, anyone who reads St. Thomas' texts for Corpus Christi day to see how far they go in separating subjective and objective forms of worship— to what extent that is, the Bread of the Sacrifice is presented more for the sake of being shown and seen than for the sake of being eaten in the Communion—anyone who does turn to the texts will find that they contain nothing of the sort. Rather, he will find to the contrary that Thomas speaks many times of *sumere* and *edere,* of *manducatio,* of *esca* and *cibus* and *saturatio,* that is of eating, of partaking, of the meal, of food, of satiety, and last but not least, of the sacrifice.

In the main, then, Thomas lived the life of a teacher, and flung his full energies and talent into the role. In the *Summa Against the Pagans,* the first great systematic sketch on which he ventured, there is a modest, oblique allusion to what he regarded as his life's task, the *propositum nostrae intentionis.* By way of effacing himself, he attributes his own manifesto to another: "To use the words of Hilary: 'I feel that I owe it to God to make this the foremost duty of my life: that all my thought and speech proclaim Him.'"[5] These words were written at the beginning of his career. And in the period shortly before his death, after ecstatic transport of some duration, he confided to his friend Reginald that he hoped to God, if his teaching and writing were now over, that the end of his life would come quickly.[6]

Augustine said of himself that he was one of those who "write as they grow and grow as they write." Thomas never spoke so directly of himself. Augustine, then, was saying that he was by nature a writer. Theodor Haecker considers this formulation virtually the definition of a writer. It remains open to question, of course, whether we have really grasped the essence of St. Augustine if we understand him principally as a writer. But I believe that if we substitute the word "teach" for "write," and if we say of Thomas that he was one of those who teach as they grow and grow as they teach, then we have fastened upon an extremely essential trait in St. Thomas. Moreover, Thomas spoke very explicitly about this matter, if not about himself; he had a great deal to say about teaching and the teacher. At this point we must say something about his theory of teaching.[7]

Teaching, says Thomas, is one of the highest manifestations of the life of the mind, for the reason that in teaching the *vita contemplativa* and the *vita activa* are joined— not just patched together superficially, not merely connected "factually," but united in a natural and necessary union. The true teacher has grasped a truth for itself, by purely receptive contemplation; he passes it on to others who likewise desire to partake of this truth. The teacher, then, looks to the truth of things; that is the contemplative aspect of teaching. It is also the aspect of silence, without which the words of the teacher would be unoriginal in the primary meaning of that word, would be empty talk, gesture, chatter, if not fraud. But the teacher simultaneously looks into the faces of living human beings— and he subjects himself to the rigorously disciplined, wearisome labor of clarifying, of presenting, of communicating. Where this communication does not take place, teaching does not take place.

Thus, the more intensively and the more passionately a man engages in these two activities, the more he is a teacher. On the one hand, there is his relationship with truth, the power of silent listening to reality; on the other hand, there is his affirmative concern for his audience and his pupils. And we may say that Thomas personally accomplished both these activities with extraordinary intensity.

The conjunction of these two things is by no means the rule. There have been great thinkers and savants who lacked the capacity to communicate in teaching, and perhaps had not the desire to do so. Goethe was one of these. In his attitude of selfless observation of the truth Goethe was closely akin to Thomas. "Let the eye be light"; "grasp objects purely"; "complete renunciation of all pretension" —Thomas would have wholly approved of these magnificent precepts of Goethe's. Nevertheless, Goethe said of himself that he was more concerned with penetrating into the nature of things than in "expressing himself in . . . speaking, transmitting, teaching." In a letter to Schiller he once wrote that the gift of teaching had been denied him.

With Thomas, on the other hand—this should really be clear from what we have already said about his love for the disputation—this concentration upon the partner in discourse, the listener, the reader and pupil, was profoundly characteristic. He devoted his best energies and the longest period of his life, not to a work of "scholarship," but to a textbook for beginners, although it was, to be sure, the fruit of the deepest absorption with Truth. The *Summa theologica* expressly sets out to be a beginner's textbook. If we did not know that Thomas had little feeling for irony, we might in fact take the preface to the *Summa theologica* for the sharpest kind of Socratic irony. For what is its general tenor but the following: there are plenty of learned books for advanced students, but there is no complete survey for beginners, *ad eruditionem incipientium*.

Precisely this characterizes the teacher, it seems to me: he possesses the art of approaching his subject from the point of view of the beginner; he is able to enter into the psychological situation of one encountering a subject for the first time. There is an element in this that goes far beyond the realm of method, of didacticism, of pedagogical skill. To put it another way, in this attitude the methodological skill which can be learned is linked with something else that probably cannot ever be learned, really.

A few things are clear about this factor: it is a fruit of love, of loving devotion to the learner, of loving identification of the teacher with the beginner. True learning, when all is as it should be, is more than mere acquisition of material. It is rather a growing into a spiritual reality which the learner cannot yet grasp as a purely intellectual matter. His uncritical, credulous link with the teacher nevertheless permits him to enter and take hold of this reality. In just this same way the teacher, insofar as he succeeds in lovingly identifying himself with the beginner, partakes of something that in the ordinary course of nature is denied to mature men: he sees the reality *just as* the beginner can see it, with all the innocence of a first encounter, and yet at the same time with the matured powers of comprehension and penetration that the cultivated mind possesses. Thomas possessed this gift in bountiful measure; and I think that the freshness of statement and the classical simplicity of diction that mark his textbook for beginners must be explained by that identification.

It must be added that Thomas combined the true teacher's love of his task with a masterly command of the didactic craft. He makes some interesting observations on the principles of that craft in the above-mentioned preface to the *Summa theologica*.[8] He points out, for example, that it is essential to avoid the aversion which is engendered by overfamiliarity and constant repetition of the same things. This does not imply that the teacher should make the subject "interesting" by hook or crook, in order to facilitate the learner's task. On the contrary, it means this: all knowledge of any depth, not only philosophizing, begins with amazement. If that is true, then everything depends upon leading the learner to recognize the amazing qualities, the *mirandum,* the "novelty" of the subject under discussion. If the teacher succeeds in doing this, he has done something more important than and quite different from making knowledge entertaining and interesting. He has, rather, put the learner on the road to genuine questioning.

And it is genuine questioning that inspires all true learning. In other words, it has dawned on the learner that what really counts is never to be taken for granted, is strange, amazing, deeper than it seems to be to common sense. That, then, is what Thomas aimed at. And in that sense, I believe, we must understand the reports of his contemporaries who testify that Thomas captivated the students of the University of Paris by the newness of his teaching ("new *articuli,*" "a new way of answering," "new arguments"—such are some of the phrases in the first biography of Thomas.[9]) This does not mean that Thomas' appeal was a faddish one. Rather the great teacher was demonstrating his thesis that the truth can only be kept alive and present in a living language which continuously grasps and puts a new stamp upon what has long been known and thought.

In the midst of the tremendous demands made upon him by his teaching, and challenged by questions shot at him from every side—in the midst of all this intellectual commotion, Thomas wrote his great systematic works. Some of them are the more or less direct fruit of his teaching itself. But his greatest systematic works, the *Summa theologica* and the *Summa Against the Pagans,* were not. His works—the sheer physical labor they represent is in itself imposing—can probably be explained in only one way: that Thomas was present in the body amid the fret and fever of those times, especially of the Parisian disputes, but that all the while he dwelt in an inner cloister of his own, that his heart was wholly untouched and untroubled, concentrated upon the totality of reality; that wrapped in the silence that filled the innermost cell of his soul he simply did not hear the din of polemics in the foreground; that he listened to something beyond it, something entirely different, which was the vital thing for him.

Perhaps we may say that several elements contributed to his imperturbability: a mystic (in the narrower sense) rapture; the capacity to give himself entirely to a subject (once, dictating at night, he simply did not notice that the candle in his hand had burned down and was singeing his fingers); and finally a concentration, acquired by schooling of the will, which made it possible for him to dictate to three or four scribes simultaneously—different texts, of course. In this way and under such conditions he produced, in a lifetime of not quite fifty years, that vast body of work which in printed editions fills thirty folio volumes.

Which are his "major works" is a question not easy to answer; it depends on what we mean by major work. Our tendency would be to relegate the *opuscula* to the background; but if by major works we mean those which had the strongest influence upon Thomas' own times, then of course the polemics belong in that category, both those written for the voluntary poverty movement and those directed against the "Averroists." In any case, some important pronouncements are to be found among the *opuscula,* for example the essay on political rule and *De ente et essentia.*

With more justification we might look for St. Thomas' "major works" among his great commentaries. Foremost among them are the twelve commentaries on Aristotle, all written in the last eight years of Thomas' life. These commentaries are the single principal document in the reception of Aristotle which transformed the intellectual outlook of the West.

Incidentally, Thomas also wrote commentaries on Scripture—on the Book of Job, on the Psalms, on Isaiah, on Jeremiah, on Matthew and John, on the Epistles of Paul. Although these commentaries contain such superlative bits as the exegesis of the prologue to the Gospel of John ("In the beginning was the Word")—an exegesis which can well be called the most magnificent of all formulations of the doctrine of the Logos to be found in Occidental theology—nevertheless I am compelled to say that these are works in which the weakness of scholastic dialectic is revealed. The Biblical texts are for the most part historical utterances and not systematic logical treatises. They cannot be reduced to the form of a syllogism. We do not take kindly to finding the fourteen epistles of St. Paul presented as a clearly arranged nexus of theses which are linked to one another logically rather than historically.

I have already spoken briefly of the *Quaestiones disputatae* and the *Quaestiones quodlibetales*. They constitute no small portion of St. Thomas' complete works; in the Latin editions they amount to sixteen hundred closely printed pages. And if by "major work" we mean a work in which the subjects of a thinker's investigations are set forth in the greatest detail, then the *Quaestiones disputatae* with their twenty to thirty arguments in each *articulus* must certainly be called major. For a time, indeed, the attention of scholars was fixed too narrowly upon the *Summa theologica*—which led to what may be called a classicistic picture of Thomas. In the *Quaestiones disputatae,* on the other hand, we encounter Thomas the "poser of problems."[10] There the *quaestiones* are really questions, dilemmas, dubieties. The *Quaestiones disputatae* frequently come to an end like the Platonic dialogues; they make no claim to offering comprehensive answers, but throw open the gates to an infinitude of further seeking.

Thus, the first article of *Quaestiones disputatae de veritate,* which examines the question: "What is truth?" is a good sample of this approach. Thomas does not arrive at a definition of truth; rather, he names several distinguishing characteristics which, however, by no means fit smoothly together; none of these characteristics is acknowledged as solely valid; none is flatly excluded. The road opens up into a boundless unknown; or more precisely, into the unfathomable, into the *mysterium.* Chenu says that the subsequent *Disputationes metaphysicae* by the later Jesuit Suarez have only the name in common with the *Quaestiones disputatae* of the thirteenth century.[11] Later scholastics so perverted the original significance of *quaestio* —question—that Descartes, say, in the title of his *Meditations,* felt called upon to disclaim any intention of writing *quaestiones.*

Among the most interesting and indeed most amusing of St. Thomas' writings are the *Quaestiones quodlibetales,* the fruit of the free discussions which Thomas was so fond of launching at the university, wherein those questions are raised which stirred his age: questions of the structure of the universe,[12] of the extent to which one should obey an erring conscience,[13] of the permissibility of holding several benefices simultaneously,[14] of the right of public criticism,[15] down to the poser, probably asked by students out of sheer high spirits (and incidentally of Biblical origin: 3 Esdras 4), which is stronger: wine, the king, woman, or truth.[16]

Finally a word on the two *summas,* the *Summa Against the Pagans* and the *Summa theologica.* Both are total accounts, and on that score alone may be called "major works." The *Summa Against the Pagans* is despite the title anything but a polemical work. That is the novelty of it; we are no longer dealing with a "crusade," but with an "encounter."[17] Naturally Thomas is concerned with demonstrating Christian truth, and therefore with refuting the *mahumetistae et pagani* to whom his words are directed. But he intends a refutation in the mode of the disputation, in which the opposing position is stated in terms of its strongest arguments—precisely in those terms.

Another characteristic must be noted of this, St. Thomas' first *summa,* written between the thirty-fourth and the thirty-eighth years of his life. Because this is directed to pagans, I cannot, he says, appeal to Holy Scriptures, neither to the Old Testament, as I would do in converse with Jews, nor to the New Testament, as in converse with heretics. It is therefore necessary "to go back to natural reason, to which all are obliged to assent, but which fails us in divine things."[18] And then he speaks, as if warning himself, of the *praesumptio comprehendendi et demonstrandi,* of the presumption of attempting to understand and to prove. Nevertheless, he attacks the mammoth task with an attitude that may perhaps be called courageous resignation of *ratio*.

The *Summa theologica,* finally, is the work on which Thomas labored for seven years, right down to his last year (though not to the time of his death), and which nevertheless was left unfinished. It is his *opus magnum;* the torso we have contains three thousand articles. The comparison with Gothic cathedrals has been cited so often that it would seem as if nothing more of value could be extracted from it. Yet anyone who understands Chartres, not merely as a piece of architecture, but as the attempt to give architectural form to the Mystery of Christ as the liberator of Creation,[19] will perceive deeper meaning in the comparison of the *Summa* with the cathedral. In its bold and, incidentally, wholly original architecture St. Thomas' *Summa* is also attempting to give embodiment to an idea. Its structure attempts to express the structure of reality as a Whole. "Reality" is at bottom not a static state, but happening, dynamics—in more precise language, history, which means event permeated by spirit and flowing out of freedom. Every systematic examination of the Whole has its dubious aspects, of course; there is the danger that this historical nature of reality will be reduced to the vanishing point by the formalistic structure of concepts and theses. But the brilliance of St. Thomas' *Summa theologica,* the quality which makes it a work of genius, is precisely that it avoids this danger. It succeeds in linking history *and* system, in projecting the nature of reality as happening *within* the orderly structure of ideas.

If we wish to reproduce adequately the structure of the *Summa,* we cannot, as in an outline, write the titles of its three parts one under the other. We must rather arrange them in a circular diagram, in a ring returning back upon itself: the outpouring of reality out of the divine Source, which by necessity contains within its initial stages the state of being on the way back to the same Source, with the Creator Who in Christ has become one with the Creation revealing Himself as the Way of this return. Early in his life's work, in the first book of his *Commentary on the Sentences,* Thomas himself declared (at the age of twenty-eight): "In the emergence of creatures from their first Source is revealed a kind of circulation, *quaedam circulatio vel regiratio,* in which all things return, as to their end, back to the very place from which they had their origin in the beginning."[20]

IX

Should we inquire about the linguistic form of the vast body of work that Thomas has bequeathed to us, the answer of course would be that the whole is written in Latin. But that would scarcely cover the case. We can go to our bookseller's and buy Cicero's *Tusculan Disputations,* St. Thomas' *Summa Against the Pagans,* and the neo-scholastic *Elementa philosophiae Aristotelico-Thomasticae.* All three works are available in modern editions; all three are "written in Latin." Between the first and the second book thirteen hundred years intervene, between the second and third six hundred and fifty years. On the basis of the time factor alone, of course, the Latin is very different indeed. But I should like to call attention to a difference of quite another character—not to differences in literary technique, or vocabulary, or grammar, or even subject matter. The *Tusculan Disputations* are obviously written in the author's native language. That is clearly not the case with the neoscholastic textbook. Cicero's Latin is living language; neoscholastic Latin is dead language.

But what is the nature of the Latin in the *Summa Against the Pagans?* It is not possible to answer this question so readily. The language in which St. Thomas wrote his books was certainly not his mother tongue; and yet this Latin was closer to him and "more natural"—infinitely so—than the neoscholastic Latin of a present-day author of a textbook of philosophy. And this was so not only because Thomas, as an Italian speaking a Romance tongue, still had Latin "in his bones," as it were, but also because medieval Latin was not yet, as present-day Latin is, an unequivocally dead language. To be sure, it was also not an unequivocally living language. The real situation is difficult to define.

If we read a thirteenth-century book written in Latin—the *Summa Against the Pagans,* say—we are more or less unconsciously under the sway of the devastating verdict which the Humanists passed upon this Latin at the beginning of the Modern Age. *Language*, in fact, was the basis on which the division of eras into Antiquity, Middle Ages, and Modern Times was originally made. The Middle Ages were regarded as the interval which lacked independent significance, the "pause," as it were, between the era of classical antiquity and the renovation and rebirth of that era among the philologists of Humanism.

Laurentius Valla, the conscientious fifteenth-century professor of rhetoric and author of the fundamental work of Humanist Latinity, *De elegantiis Latinae linguae,* decreed that the "first scholastic," Boethius, was the first man to have spoken and written that "barbarous" Latin.[1] Even for Hegel the language was still the great blight that lay upon medieval philosophy. It would be, he says, "asking too much of anyone" to read these works, for they are "as prolix as they are paltry, terribly written and voluminous."[2]

In recent decades philology has to some extent amended this verdict—although present opinions are greatly varied indeed. Thus, for example, we are told that medieval Latin continued to grow "just as, in popular belief, the hair and nails of the dead go on growing";[3] or that it is in some ways like a water nymph "who through secret union with a chosen man obtains real, viable children";[4] or that it is like an animal in a cage, lacking freedom, having no real opportunity for development, but still capable of rearing up and displaying its native strength.[5] But it has also been said that the dignity, the importance, and the vitality of Latin lie precisely in its being "the language of a community of ideas,"[6] "the mother tongue of the Occident,"[7] "the language of tradition."[8]

The most competent, intelligent, and well-founded words on this subject have recently been said by the Dutch philologist Christine Mohrmann in her treatise on the dualism of medieval Latin.[9] By dualism she means that medieval Latin did not only live on the heritage of classical antiquity; that it derived its vitality chiefly—and this, modern philology inclines to overlook or underestimate—out of the active life of the Christian community, especially its liturgy.[10] The conclusion Christine Mohrmann arrives at is that Latin was *une langue vivante sans être la langue d'une communauté ethnique*[11]—a living language in spite of not being the language of an ethnic community. In other words, a language that went on developing in a living manner. Medieval men were not concerned with the restoration but with the utilization of the classical heritage.[12] Latin *became* a dead language only after classicism had won out and had installed Cicero's Latin as a venerated museum piece "guarded by worshipful conservators, the Humanists and the classical philologists."[13]

The Humanists fancied that they were doing something wholly aristocratic in bringing back classical Latin. In reality they were engaged in a slavish imitation, a "servile reproduction" of the Latin of the past.[14] The worst of it was that precisely this procedure sealed the death of the Latin language. After all, French, like all the other modern Romance languages, arose out of a kind of pidgin Latin, out of the most un-Ciceronian everyday Latin of merchants and soldiers—which did not keep French from becoming an extremely vital, cultivated, and highly differentiated language. The trouble with Humanist Latin was that it separated speech from life, and from the life of the mind also—whereas the Latin of scholasticism remained always a living language, *la langue vivante de l'Université*.[15]

These matters are of great importance for a correct understanding of St. Thomas. Quite unlike contemporary neoscholasticism, which refers back to him and claims to bring his doctrine up to date, Thomas was not writing a dead and artificial language, but a natural and living language. We may also say: Thomas spoke a language; he did not "employ a terminology"!

To be sure, this language of St. Thomas cannot be described simply as "medieval Latin." That term is far too sweeping; it takes in poetry from the time of Venantius Fortunatus through the compositions of Alcuin, Roswitha von Gandersheim, and Hildegard von Bingen to Francis of Assisi's *Hymn to Brother Sun;* it encompasses philosophical and theological prose from Boethius to Anselm to Bonaventura and Duns Scotus. Moreover, it also embraces the *spoken* word—spoken not only in divine services, but also in solemn judicial or political decrees, in sermons, in international diplomacy, and incidentally in song also (the *carmina burana* were, after all, not meant to be read!). Within this vast realm the phrase *la langue vivante de l'Université* marks off a considerably smaller circle.

Thomas speaks the Latin of the university, of the schools, of scholasticism at its apogee. His was the language of teaching, and hence a language directed primarily toward clarification, toward lucidity, toward preventing misunderstandings. In saying this, of course, we are naturally defining a limit, a limitation in purely linguistic terms. One hundred years before St. Thomas that cosmopolitan gentleman John of Salisbury wrote a far more elegant Latin, with stylistic flourishes and occasional sallies of ironic wit. By Thomas' time all that has disappeared, as has the language shaped by mystic emotion of the great canons of St. Victor. In its stead there appears a language aiming totally at statement of the substance, renouncing all musicality. This is the *lingua Parisiensis*— which, incidentally, another great Humanist, Pico della Mirandola, commended in the following terms: "It is possible," he said, "that your somewhat dry language is offensive to the ear; but the intellect accepts it because it is closer to reality."[16] Closer than the musical elegance cultivated in Florence, he probably means.

Along with this attribute of the language of the schools —the concern with clarity and nothing but clarity—there is another tendency and a fairly dangerous one: the inclination this language has to become "technical," that is to say, a kind of jargon wherein words are stamped with special meanings. "Heat" is of course a word in use in the ordinary, general language; but when physics textbooks speak of "heat" they are using a word which has a place in a fixed terminology. They mean something that the ordinary user of the word may not even understand. Wherever people attempt to speak with the greatest possible unambiguity, they are inclined to abandon the natural language and to substitute a "terminology." In scholastic Latin the case was no different. But it can be said, I believe, that Thomas—perhaps alone among the great scholastics—saw the danger of this tendency and as far as possible opposed it. There is no doubt about his absolute resolve to avoid ambiguity; he was not seeking mellifluousness, not "poetry." But he greatly mistrusted artificial, contrived language; he mistrusted mere terminology.

There is a third statement which must be made about the language of the medieval universities, scholastic Latin: it was to a large extent a translating language, and therefore was necessarily an unoriginal language. In the realm of philosophy and theology Latin had always been a dependent language; the great writers among the Romans used to demonstrate their linguistic talent by dint of translating from the Greek. Cicero, for example, translated the Greek word *atom,* individual particle, by the Latin word *individuum. Contemplatio* was found as the equivalent for *theoria.* Seneca, also a great translator, complained that to find adequate formulations for philosophical subject matter a Roman had constantly to maltreat and twist words; he was worried that there existed no Latin word to express what Plato and Aristotle had called *to on,* that which is.[17] It is therefore an old complaint that Latin, as soon as it deals principally with philosophy, becomes a translating language. The Roman Boethius, who had completed his studies in Athens and conceived the plan of making all of Plato and all of Aristotle available to the Latin West by translation and commentary, continued this time-hallowed effort. *Principium, actus, universale, subjectum, definitio,* and many other words now completely familiar to us were first given their special senses and co-ordinated with Greek prototypes by Boethius.

But Boethius had succeeded in translating only a very small part of the works of Aristotle. Now, at the end of the twelfth century, the whole of Aristotle fell within the purview of the Latin West. Aristotelian metaphysics, ethics, psychology became available. All this now had to be translated. The first task was the simple one of "carrying across," conveying the substance, so that readers of Latin could have some idea of what Aristotle had said and what he meant. In the course of this enterprise scholastic Latin, the language of the university, assumed its final form.

The sealing took place in an inevitably violent manner. There simply was not time enough for organic growth. And we must consider that it was not Plato, say, who had to be translated, not the poetical Plato who in his dialogues had taken up and given a sovereign polish to the ordinary language of simple men. It was the austere, sober schoolmaster Aristotle. And the naturally unphilosophical language of the Romans was the medium through which these works had to be mastered and assimilated. Much is said about the "penetration" of Aristotelian writing—as though this were a process which took place of its own accord, with the alert minds of the era merely looking on. The process was hardly so passive. Rather, these very minds were engaged in tremendous activity; there was no "penetration," but active appropriation. The act of translating meant that the best thinkers of the time were taking possession of a most highly differentiated instrument, and were learning to manipulate it.[18]

St. Thomas, then, worked within the area of this medieval, and more especially, scholastic Latin whose outlines we have sketched. Nevertheless, as speaker and writer he remained a unique figure and in no way to be confounded with any of his contemporaries. It is forever stirring, when one turns abruptly from St. Augustine to St. Thomas—from the one to the other of these two great doctors of Christendom—to see how far removed Thomas is from Augustine.

"Too late I loved Thee, O Thou Beauty of ancient days, yet ever new! Too late I loved Thee! And behold, Thou wert within, and I abroad, and there I searched for Thee; deformed I, plunging amid those fair forms which Thou hadst made. Thou wert with me, but I was not with Thee. Things held me far from Thee, which, unless they were in Thee, were not at all. Thou calledst, and shoutedst, and burstest my deafness. . . . Thou touchedst me, and I burned for Thy peace."[19] That is Augustine. There is nothing of this sort in the whole of St. Thomas' works. Thomas does not have that brilliance of style, that verbal grace, that music; neither does he have that personal tone. We have no difficulty sensing the living human being behind the words of Augustine, the man who speaks "now," out of a particular state of mind. Thomas, on the other hand, cannot be recognized behind his words; his words are like crystal formations, and the thought does not leap to our minds that they, too, have sprung from a mother liquor.

No one would wish to assert that Augustine's phraseology is unclear; it often possesses an insurpassable exactness. But at bottom Thomas wishes to communicate something else entirely, and that alone; he wishes to make plain, not his own inner state, but his insight into a given subject. Such an aim does not, of course, exclude grandeur of form; it does not exclude beauty. And that austere kind of beauty is certainly found in the writings of Thomas. There are numerous indications, moreover, that Thomas strove for such beauty. Take the following sentence from the *Summa Against the Pagans*: "They hold a plainly false opinion who say that in regard to the truth of religion it does not matter what a man thinks about the Creation so long as he has the correct opinion concerning God. . . . An error concerning the Creation ends as false thinking about God"—*sic ergo patet falsam esse quorundam sententiam, qui dicebant nihil interesse ad fidei veritatem, quid de creaturis quisque sentiret, dummodo circa Deum recte sentiatur . . .: nam error circa creaturas redundat in falsam de Deo sententiam.*[20] This sentence, it seems to me, has a distinct kinship to the last bars of a Bach organ fugue. Beauty of language, then, certainly exists in the works of Thomas. But it is not really the beauty of a work of art. This language is beautiful as a perfect tool is beautiful.

Nevertheless, Thomas never regarded language as a mere tool. This is, I think, a point of some importance, and of some topical importance as well. In the realm of philosophizing, governed as it is by logic and deduction, we frequently come up against the opinion that human language is a tool like a hammer or a drill, a tool of communication; and if this tool should not quite meet one's needs, it is simply repaired or exchanged for another. In principle that does not sound like a bad idea. But I must put the matter somewhat more plainly: in some quarters the opinion prevails that the natural, historical language, the product of normal growth, has largely proved to be an unsuitable tool—for philosophical uses, at any rate. Hence this unsuitable tool must be exchanged for a more suitable one, in order to rescue meaning in general; it must be replaced, that is, by an artificial language based on convention, one which employs symbols instead of natural words.

I think it highly important to show that on this point

Thomas held a different opinion, and that his position involved a principle of the highest importance. The question hangs upon the relationship between the natural, historical language and a synthetic technical jargon based on convention—the relationship, as I have said earlier, between language and terminology. As a matter of fact it is often denied that there is any difference in principle between language and terminology. All speech, it is argued, deals with arbitrarily alterable, exchangeable "tools" which may be used at discretion, *ad placitum*. As far as the concept of "tool" is concerned, incidentally, we must distinguish between the *instrumentum coniunctum* and the *instrumentum separatum,* between the tool directly connected with the user and the tool apart from him. The hand is an *instrumentum coniunctum,* the hammer an *instrumentum separatum.*

Thomas himself, to be sure, did not bring up this matter when he discussed the relationship between natural language and artificial terminology; but it is true to his spirit to say that the natural, historical, normally developed language is, like the hand, an *instrumentum coniunctum*.[21] And from this three conclusions spring. First, we obviously cannot ourselves make it, like a hammer. Second, we cannot arbitrarily change it, which means that we are dependent upon it and that its inherent qualities are binding upon us. And third, we can use (and understand) even an artificial terminology only with the aid and on the basis of the natural language, just as we need the hand in order to handle a hammer. All this leads to the following conclusion: terminology draws its life from the natural, historical language; this language remains the obligatory foundation for all communication, whereas a terminology is not binding in the same way.

I do not say that terminology cannot be something

highly meaningful and practical, and even inevitable—above all in the realms of science. When the physician says *exitus* he is referring, very precisely, to a clearly defined physiological process—"precise" in the sense of cut off, cut out, artificially separated from the fullness of reality. The word in the natural language co-ordinate with the technical term *exitus* is "death." This word does *not* mean something precise; it takes in the total process, including the physiological fact, but including also many things beyond that; it embraces the wide reality of what really takes place when someone dies: the end of the *status viatoris,* for good or ill; the loss of father, child, wife—and a number of other things that perhaps are scarcely definable. All this, in other words the Whole, is present in the word "death"—including the incomprehensibility of it; and all these things are audible only to one who participates, hearing and speaking, in the living language. The word "death" will not lend itself to being contracted and abridged to a partial meaning. Because it is not "precise" (cut off)—for that very reason it is more to the point, more accurate, than the technical term. And pre-eminently in the realm of philosophy we are dealing with fundamental matters which reflect the Whole of the universe and of existence: happiness, death, love, truth, reality, life, and so on.

In regard to St. Thomas' position, there are two points to be made, one negative and one positive. To take the negative first: despite first appearances, Thomas has no real terminology. An extremely detailed investigation has been made, which demonstrates this with complete clarity.[22] Thomas did not establish any definite, fixed terms which he planned to use in a consistent manner. On the contrary, he was fond of employing several synonymous expressions side by side.[23] We find that he employs no less than ten different phrases to express the concept of relation.[24] Contrariwise, the word *forma* has ten different meanings as Thomas used it.[25] *Causa efficiens* is at one time *causa effectiva,* another time *causa agens* or *activa* or *movens.*[26] Not only is this his practice, but it is intentionally so. Thomas wanted it that way. It was, as Blanche says, not a mere chance matter of temperament, but the product of definite, clearly formulated principles. Thomas was careful to avoid making exact, "precise" definitions of such fundamental concepts as "cognition" or "truth."[27] For Thomas was convinced that an absolutely adequate name, completely and exhaustively defining a given subject or situation so that all alternatives are excluded and that name alone can be employed, simply cannot exist. Chenu formulated his view in these words: *La clarté des mots ne lui dissimule pas le mystère des choses*—the clearness of the terms does not disguise from him the mystery in the things.[28]

Secondly, and this on the positive side, we must comment: the decisive factor for Thomas was never the definition as some one thinker had given it, even if the thinker was himself. Rather, the decisive factor was linguistic usage, *usus,* which is to say, the living speech of human beings. He propounded this view many times—usually, incidentally, linking it with a reference to Aristotle. Aristotle, too, followed the same procedure, and he too put it in so many words: "In the naming of things one must go with the crowd."[29]

Of course it is not easy to describe usage, the living speech of men. Obviously the category does not include defective, trivial, impoverished, careless, slangy speech of the streets (although it has been observed that Thomas does not always reject even an incorrect colloquial use of a word).[30] When we say "usage," we mean the speech of men who are "cultivated" in the best sense and who draw sustenance from the living roots of the language. This no doubt includes the language of poets, and even a poet's linguistic innovations, so long as these are consonant with the spirit of the language. On the other hand this definition of usage rules out cut-and-dried jargon severed from the roots of the language. (Nowadays such jargon is beginning more and more to invade all forms of public utterance—a dangerous development which not only poisons the purity of language but cripples the human capacity to approach and express the deeper dimensions of the universe in general, or even to observe them.)

Thus Thomas says: *nominibus utendum est ut plures utuntur*—we must use names as they are generally used.[31] That is to say, we should not arbitrarily coin new names, or employ existing names in arbitrary new meanings. Moreover, in investigating the meaning of such fundamental words as "justice" we ought to look into the living usage of the language. (The usage—not the etymology! I think that Heidegger's procedure of determining the meaning of fundamental words from their etymology is demonstrably fruitless, if not misleading.) This is the maxim that Thomas himself obeys.

He asks, for example: What do people mean when they say "similar"? It would seem at first sight that we might rest content with the definition to be found in philosophical dictionaries. Does it not sound perfectly obvious to say that two things are "like" one another when they agree in all characteristics, and "similar" to one another when a portion of their characteristics are in agreement? Such a statement seems to cover the matter. But Thomas is not satisfied with it. He examines usage, which manifests itself in the multiplicity of actual possibilities for the employment of a word, or in the impossibility of employing it in a particular context. Thus, Thomas points out, it is impossible to say that the father is similar to his son—from which it becomes clear that the concept of similarity contains something different from what we would be led to suspect by that apparently so exact definition, namely, an element of derivation, descent, origin.[32]

Now we may ask what law prevents us from saying nevertheless that the father is similar to his son? That is difficult to say. Yet a kind of law is there. And Thomas acknowledges it. In so doing he concedes that in natural, historical human speech there is something which we cannot manipulate at will as we can things and tools which we have made—something which we have no right to deal with arbitrarily.

We have still to comment on Thomas' special, personal style of language and speech. Thomas seems to agree with Goethe in that, faced with the choice, he will always prefer the less "inflated" expression.[33] He avoids unusual and ostentatious phraseology. That has its disadvantages, of course. Unadorned, dry clarity can be tedious. In the case of St. Thomas we must imagine that this danger was alleviated not only by the tempo of delivery, but also by the gesticulations that no doubt accompanied his speech. We must think of both, gesticulations and tempo, as southern Italian in character. But perhaps that is not especially important.

An outstanding trait of St. Thomas' style is, it seems to me, its sobriety. By that, of course, I do not mean dullness or lack of animation, incapacity for enthusiasm or want of energy. Rather, I mean the firm rejection and avoidance of everything that might conceal, obscure, or distort reality. I mean extreme receptivity to reality, unencumbered by any sort of subjectivity; I mean the concern to frame everything, and only those things, which can stand up to a regard wholly without illusions.

Ernst Jünger has spoken of a kind of courage which

he calls "two-o'clock-in-the-morning bravery." There is also something like a two-o'clock-in-the-morning sensitivity to "dicta," especially to *"pious* dicta." It seems to me that even in such a mood we can still read an *articulus* by St. Thomas. And I have a notion that he rather intended his written words to stand up to such a disillusioned gaze. That accounts for his dogged resistance to everything that is merely well said, to all pretentious airs about himself and his work—and even to specifically "religious" terminology. The word "religious" must be put in quotation marks here, for in reality this very abstinence from a "religious" vocabulary has its origin in a religious point of view. St. Thomas' language is devoid of *unctio,* unctiousness. Bonaventura, undoubtedly with a glance at his colleague Thomas, remarked that among the Franciscans *unctio* came first and only then *speculatio,* but that with the Dominicans it was the reverse.[34] *Unctio* is lacking, I have said. Strictly speaking, this cannot really be stated so definitely; what is "lacking" is the visible and audible, perhaps only the customary, expression of religious emotion.

But who can say whether this lack is not founded upon an equanimity which springs from a reverence all the deeper? Thomas' characteristic distaste for "religious short-circuits," his rational sobriety, undoubtedly has religious if not mythical roots. We define a thing, he once said, not by its ultimate principle, but by the proximate one;[35] and therefore the answer to the question, "What is the essence of virtue?" is not "Virtue is that which God desires," but "Virtue means to do what is consonant with insight and appropriate to the situation."

Out of that same unshakable sobriety Thomas—although in reality he was so "modern" that it made many of his brethren and colleagues dizzy to behold his flights—refused to become involved in the topical "religious" concerns which agitated his own era. For example, he completely ignored the talk, so general at the time, about his century's eschatological character—this although the generals of both the Franciscan and the Dominican Orders had issued (in 1256) a joint circular letter concerning the apocalyptic meaning of the two mendicant orders. *They,* the mendicants, the letter asserted, were the two witnesses of Christ clothed in sackcloth, the two stars of the Sibyls, and so on.[36] A year later Thomas made the matter-of-fact statement: "No one span of time can be named, neither a small nor a great one, after which the end of the world is to be expected."[37]

We have said that Thomas' sobriety arose from his total preoccupation with the truth of reality. There was something else connected with it, something characteristic of Thomas and of his way of speaking and writing, namely, his remarkable inner independence. Sometimes this independence amounted to a boldness that stopped at nothing. Thus he once asks himself, in his commentary on the Book of Job, whether Job's candid speech to God did not occasionally depart from the respect due to the Lord.[38] To which he counters: "Truth does not change because of the high dignity of him to whom it is addressed; he who speaks the truth cannot be overcome, no matter with whom he disputes."

X

To epitomize the intellectual task confronting Thomas, and which he set for himself, I must use the image of Odysseus' bow, which was so difficult to bend that it took almost superhuman strength to draw the ends closer together. I have said that almost as soon as Thomas awoke to critical consciousness he recognized that it was his life's task to join these two extremes which seemed inevitably to be pulling away from one another. And I have labeled the extremes, in a highly inadequate simplification, "Aristotle" on the one hand and the "Bible" on the other hand. The name "Aristotle" was meant to serve as a cryptic word for natural reality as a whole, for the visible, sense-perceived world of physical, material things and—within man himself—for sensuousness, for nature and naturalness, and also for the natural cognitive powers of reason, the *lumen naturale*. The other cue word, "Bible," was meant to include the whole realm of the supernatural: the suprarationality of divine revelation; the reality of universe, man, and God which is accessible only in faith; the Gospel's doctrine of salvation as the norm of human life.

But the man who undertook this task of joining the two was Thomas Aquinas. This means that it was undertaken by a man of almost unparalleled power of mind, a man whose scope, precision, and vigor in clarification of ideas are seldom to be met with in the history of human thought. He approached this task with penetrating insight into the substance of the questions. And for this very reason it had to become apparent from the start—could not, at least, remain hidden from Thomas himself—that his endeavor was fraught with a multitude of potential conflicts; that it would be a source of virtually incalculable difficulties and discords which could scarcely ever be brought to a final "harmony."

Thomas could no longer possess the magnificent naïveté of Boethius, who had first formulated the principle *fidem rationemque coniunge*. This Roman, wholly at home in Greek cosmology, heir to the full richness of the classical heritage, sharing the belief of Plotinus that he could venture a synthesis of Platonic and Aristotelian thought, considered it possible to discuss the Trinitarian God *without* resorting to the revealed word of Holy Scripture. His book on the Trinity contains not a single quotation from the Bible. Similarly, the simplification practiced by Anselm of Canterbury, two hundred years before Thomas, had by the thirteenth century become impossible. That mystical theologian, completely absorbed in meditation upon revealed truth, could maintain that Christian belief so completely concurred with natural reason that it could be proved on compelling rational grounds, by *rationes necessariae*.

These two potential simplifications were closed to Thomas. He could not be so "naïve." Several things had happened within Western Christendom itself which ruled out any rapid, premature harmonization. Most of all, the danger of secularization in doctrine had made its appearance in unmistakable form. That is to say, reason was threatening to separate itself from faith, to declare its independence, and to reject all suprarational and superhuman standards. This threat, moreover, was arising within Christendom itself—for example, in the circle around the Hohenstaufen Emperor, Frederick II, with whose members Thomas was personally acquainted. Peter of Hibernia, who had introduced Thomas to Aristotle while Thomas was a student at the imperial university of Naples, was another representative of this tendency. Trends such as these—and Thomas had opened his mind to them with complete lack of bias—would not allow him to simplify the problem at hand in an unjustifiably "naïve" manner.

On the other hand, his knowledge of these things and his exposure to this school of thought made him aware of the truly deadly peril which was brewing for the intellectual life of the Christian world, the peril of a split in consciousness, as it were. And perhaps there could be discerned, very far off on the horizon, the danger of a complete de-Christianization, of a secularization which would sweep forward unchecked by any psychological barriers. At any rate, the danger of a division of intellectual life into what men "knew," on the one hand, and what they "believed," on the other—a division so sharp that it would no longer be possible to maintain a bridge from the one realm to the other—had already become acute. Perhaps we can call this the catchword: the danger of "double truth." And Thomas could not possibly overlook it.

The task presented by the age itself, then, was this: to effect a legitimate union between the two realms that threatened to break apart by their own mutual repulsion. A "legitimate union" would mean two things. First, it would mean joining the two realms so that their distinctiveness and irreducibility, their relative autonomy, their intrinsic justification, were seen and recognized. Second, it would mean making their unity, their compatibility, and the necessity for their conjunction apparent not from the point of view of either of the two members of the union —neither simply from the point of view of faith nor simply from that of reason—but by going back to a deeper root of both.

In other words, the generation of the mid-thirteenth century could no longer abide by earlier answers to the problem of *fidem rationemque coniunge*. The real dichotomy had come to the fore in all its urgency; they had to come to terms with it. And Thomas undertook this task.

From the point of view of thirteenth-century "orthodoxy"—by which I mean the inevitably "moderate" climate of "prevailing" philosophical and theological ideas— the attitude of St. Thomas was aggressively unusual and disturbing. For he accepted the opposing positions, both of them, in all their radicality. More than unusual, his affirmation of the ideal of "evangelical perfection" was revolutionary—the more so since that ideal had arisen within the heretical Waldensian voluntary poverty movement, which all *bien-pensants* regarded with extreme suspicion.

Even more offensive was his resolute appeal to "Aristotle"; despite all official warnings and bans his fidelity to Aristotle was open and unbroken. And what did this mean but that he was intrepidly affirming the whole of natural reality, not only with regard to objective existence, but also *within* man himself—affirming, therefore, what Christendom's traditional sense of values subsumed under the term "the world." "They arrogated to themselves divine wisdom, although worldliness is far more native to their minds"—we have already referred to this charge which was soon raised against Albert and Thomas. Thomas attacks the kernel of this charge by analyzing the Biblical concept of "the world." There are, he says in his commentary on the Gospel of John, three different meanings of the word "world" as it is used in Holy Scripture, two of which are entirely positive.[1] "World" means, first of all, the equivalent of "creation," the whole of the things and beings created by God. Secondly, "world" can be used to mean creation newly created and liberated by Christ. However, Biblical usage may also use the phrase "the world" with pejorative overtones: in this sense "the world" stands for the inversion of the order of creation which has come about with the passage of time. Thomas speaks out against the equating of this negative concept of "world" with the first meaning (world as the whole of created things and beings). It would be understating the case to assert that Thomas "defends" natural reality; to his mind it would be utterly ridiculous for man to undertake to defend the creation. Creation needs no justification. The order of creation is, on the contrary, precisely the standard which must govern man's every judgment of things and of himself.

It is not by chance that Thomas poses to himself the following objection: Since God is an incorporeal Being and since our goal must be "likeness to God," surely it must be said that the soul separated from the body is more like God than the soul united with the body. Here is an argument that is based upon a very sublime thought with which, so it would seem, nobody can disagree. But Thomas is that nobody. He boldly contends: "The soul united with the body is more like God than the soul separated from the body because it (the soul in the body) possesses its nature in more complete fashion."[2] Corporeality, therefore, is good.

Included within this statement is a further premise: Sensuality is good (so much so that Thomas calls "unsensuality" not merely a defect, but a *vitium,* a moral deficiency);[3] anger is good;[4] sexuality is good.[5] We might cite hundreds of such sentences. Once Thomas refers to several Fathers of the Church who held that the reproduction of the human race in Paradise must have taken place in some nonsexual manner. With utter calmness, objectivity, but also absolute firmness, St. Thomas replies: *Hoc non dicitur rationabiliter,* "This cannot be said reasonably; for what belongs to the nature of man is neither taken from him nor given to him by reason of sin."[6]

Naturally such a statement has enormous consequences, above all for our fundamental conceptions of ethical conduct. If there are certain realms of objective reality which are in themselves "bad," "base," and "tainting," then it is an easy matter to determine what is good and what is bad. Virtue, for instance, would consist in avoiding such "impure" aspects of reality, such as sex. But if there are no such tainting aspects of reality, what, we may ask, is unchastity? The treatise on chastity and temperance in the *Summa theologica* strikes us as a breath of fresh air. Here is not the slightest trace of the narrowness, pettiness, and unnaturalness so common to moralistic tracts. This can only be explained by Thomas' utter fidelity to his thesis of the goodness of all created things.

Thomas' personal life, too, was marked by the same kind of tolerance and absence of prejudice. Theodor Haecker in his *Journal in the Night*[7] (July 3, 1942) has remarked: "Thomas had no thorn in the flesh."[8] Apparently Haecker did not mean this remark as sheer praise, for he added: "that explains why he is so strange and foreign to modern man."[9] I think that this strangeness, this alien quality, is in fact connected with the deepest secret of Thomas as a human being.

Perhaps one aspect of that secret is contained in the curious episode which has come down to us under the name of "the angel's girdling." Thomas himself told the story to his friend Reginald during the last period of his life. After he had been imprisoned, at the age of nineteen or twenty, his brothers sent a bejeweled courtesan to visit Thomas in his cell, to lure him from his resolve to become a mendicant friar. After he had rather roughly shown this damsel the door, Thomas fell into a deep, exhausted sleep, from which he awakened with a cry. He had cried out because in his dream an angel had girdled him in an extremely painful manner, in order to make him henceforth invulnerable to all temptations toward impurity. Whatever interpretation we may put upon this story, it is certain that Thomas—like Goethe, incidentally—always maintained that purity was a necessary condition for recognizing truth, for seeing reality. More than that, he fulfilled this condition in his own person. He was, it appears, a person of such unusual "simplicity,"[10] and this "singleness of eye" gives him such "light," that we are no doubt justified in speaking of charisma.

In this attitude of his, two elements were combined which are usually in contradiction. On the one hand, his vision remained unclouded, his judgment unconfused, above all not confused by the interpolations of his own desires. But he never assumed the mantle of the ascetic who forces his nature to renounce the world. Rather (and here comes the "on the other hand"), he was known for his hearty affirmation of all reality, especially of the world of the senses and its beauties. This union of wholehearted affirmation, on the one hand, and utterly unclouded, utterly cool clarity of vision, on the other hand—this conjunction within the mind of a man who moreover lived undemandingly in evangelical poverty was, so I believe, the fruit of an unusual, we may also say, a saintly purity.

We may well assume that such vigorous acceptance of the natural world would in some way color Thomas' approach as theologian. Two examples may serve to point up the originality of his approach to theological matters.

Albert the Great and Bonaventura had contrived, by employing an apparatus of somewhat forced symbolisms, to co-ordinate the seven Sacraments with the seven deadly sins, so that each of the seven Sacraments could be considered a cure for a specific sin. Thomas, however, argued that the establishment and the growth of the New Life takes place after the image of the life of the body: Baptism corresponds to begetting and birth, Confirmation to the attainment of puberty; Holy Communion is the nourishment of the New Life; the Sacrament of Penance is the cure for injuries and disease—and so on.[11]

Second example: the inner style of the Scriptural commentaries. The commentary on the Book of Job is considered most typical of Thomas. In order to understand its importance we must know that the theology of the time was dominated by the commentary on Job written by Gregory the Great, which indeed is magnificent in its practical wisdom. But as an interpretation of the book itself, this older commentary is pure allegorization, constantly doing violence to the text. (The seven sons of Job are first equated with the seven virtues; secondly, they "mean" the twelve Apostles. How can seven sons mean twelve Apostles? The answer is simple: seven is 3 plus 4, and twelve is 3 times 4![12] And so on.) Thomas, on the other hand, approaches the Book of Job in terms of the direct meaning of the text, as a lesson on the destiny of man and on Divine Providence.

Another feature of Thomas' must be noted here. In order to clarify Holy Scripture, he brings to bear, with superb confidence, the whole of his intellectual stock; in this commentary on the Book of Job he quotes Averroës, Avicenna, Porphyry, Pliny, Cicero, Plato, and of course, above all, Aristotle. Acceptance of all natural reality necessarily involves the acceptance of valuable insights wherever they may be found—and, therefore, also in the pre-Christian and extra-Christian worlds.

From the early decades of the thirteenth century on, as I have said, things had begun to diverge, to move vigorously apart: the Biblical and evangelical impulses on the one hand, and the exclusively philosophical and secular impulses on the other hand. It must be admitted that the work of Thomas seemed at first to feed this tendency. Thomas' very efforts to demonstrate that a more deeply grounded union was both meaningful and necessary appeared to intensify the danger of mutual isolation, to push things to extremes, and lay the groundwork for conflict. For Thomas granted the rightness of both directions, after all; each one, it would seem, could appeal to his sanction. Most of all, extreme Aristotelianism was encouraged and reinforced by the fact that St. Thomas turned so resolutely to the same Aristotle. We are told that Siger of Brabant, who was one of Thomas' most vigorous opponents during the latter's last years of teaching in Paris, had drawn many of his ideas from Thomas.[13]

The name Siger of Brabant conjures up one of those dramatic biographies with which the history of medieval philosophy is studded. A Walloon by birth, fifteen to twenty years younger than Thomas, he early became a canon of St. Martin's in Liège and then, still extremely young, a magister in the Faculty of Arts in Paris. Siger was not yet thirty when he stepped into the public arena in a tremendous dispute that threatened to split the faculty. Van Steenberghen, who has written an imposing monograph upon Siger of Brabant, summarizes his career as follows: "A young ringleader without scruples, resolved to put his point of view across with all the means at his command"; fiery of temperament, vehement, inclined to go to extremes.[14] This man, then, was teaching at the University of Paris and writing a considerable number of books, above all commentaries on Aristotle. He was constantly involved in doctrinal disputes; when summoned to appear before an Inquisitional tribunal he fled from France and appealed directly to the Pope. In Orvieto, the city which was then the seat of the Curia, he was stabbed to death by his own secretary, his career thus cut short at the age of forty.

Siger of Brabant became the spokesman for a school of thought which had become established in Paris around 1265 and which is usually referred to in the literature as

"Latin Averroism."[15] The special doctrines that Siger and his circle advocated are not the important matter for us. What is important is that these men understood and propounded Aristotle in such a manner that from the start they felt themselves exempt from any concern with the truth of the Christian revelation. Gilson has called this basic attitude "philosophism."[16] The word means two things: first, the thesis that philosophizing is in principle independent of and separate from theology and faith. For the first time in the history of Christendom the principle of uniting *ratio* and *fides,* which had been established since the days of Augustine and Boethius, was formally abrogated—abrogated, moreover, by clerical teachers at the most important academy of Christendom itself. Secondly, this newly autonomous philosophy—in defiance of the definition of its name ("search for wisdom") which had been held valid since Pythagoras—was considered to be wisdom itself, a doctrine of salvation. "There is no state superior to the practice of philosophy"—such was one of its tenets.[17]

This radical view was received with open arms at the University of Paris. And none of the great men who might effectively have opposed it was on the scene. Albert the Great was trudging all over the Western world as superior of the order and emissary of the Pope. Bonaventura had already left the university in 1257, having been called to the post of general of the Franciscan Order. Thomas had been in Italy since 1259. An English historian has characterized the situation at the University of Paris around 1268 as follows: If the group around Siger of Brabant had continued to hold the intellectual leadership unhindered, without meeting resistance, the authorities would have been compelled to close the university.[18] Perhaps that is putting the matter somewhat too strongly; but obviously the situation in Paris was speedily moving toward a crisis.

That very year of 1268 Thomas, contrary to all custom, was sent to the University of Paris for the second time. He found there not only the group of heterodox Aristotelians around Siger of Brabant, although they were his most dangerous opponents—most dangerous for him personally, too, and the opponents with whom he was forever being confounded. Confounded by whom? We must not forget that a traditional theology still existed. It was inherited from the previous century and was to a degree still dominant, still controlling the "bureaucracy" and largely determining the attitudes of the Christian world, against which Thomas tried to win recognition for his "worldliness" which, as we have said, had been inspired by his acquaintance with Aristotle and which referred back to Aristotle.

This traditional mode of seeing and interpreting the world, which has been roughly labeled with the imprecise name of "medieval Augustinism," had always harbored suspicions of everything connected with the name of Aristotle—and therefore of Thomas. These suspicions were confirmed by the kind of Aristotelianism advocated by Siger of Brabant and by his fellow polemicists, some of whom went even further than he did. For their Aristotelianism certainly verged on heresy, if it was not heresy outright.

Bonaventura, who, in his early works, had likewise been enamored of Aristotle, was disturbed. Alarmed for the unity of the Christian world view, he once more intervened in the doctrinal disputes, likewise issuing warnings. To be exact, his warning was directed against the very ideas that Thomas, undeterred, was proclaiming to be the true solution to the difficulty. And the theology of these traditionalists, wholly reverting back as it did to an interpretation of the universe which could no longer satisfy the demands of the century—this crabbedness of the traditionalists in its turn exacerbated the extremism of the men around Siger of Brabant.

This was the situation Thomas came into. Of course he was compelled to defend his position from two sides—and likewise compelled, by the struggle on two fronts, to formulate this position more precisely, to clarify it. He had still some five years to live, and was to be in Paris for a good three of them. When he left Paris after Easter in 1272, aged forty-seven, he was an exhausted man. Even if we pass over the great disputations and his regular teaching work, even if we consider only the literary output of those three years, it is well-nigh unbelievable that a single human being could have produced so much: twelve major commentaries on Aristotle, the commentary on John, the elucidation of the Epistles of Paul, the voluminous *Quaestiones disputatae* on evil, on the virtues, on the Incarnation, finally the Second Part of the *Summa theologica;* in addition to polemics, and not only against Siger of Brabant, but also in defense of the voluntary poverty movement, the very principles of which were under attack.

What chiefly interests us here is that Thomas was compelled to defend and clarify his position, based as it was on the joint affirmation of both the "Bible" and "Aristotle." And, simplifying somewhat, he was fighting a battle against the absolutizing of Aristotle, on the one hand, and against the exclusiveness of a supranaturalistic Biblicism, on the other hand. This clarification and defense, which forms the thread of all the above-mentioned works, can be reduced to a few basic lines of argument.

First, Thomas demonstrated that affirmative acceptance of the natural reality of the world and of the natural reality in man himself can be ultimately established and justified only in theological terms. The natural things of the world have a real, self-contained intrinsic being precisely by reason of having been created, precisely because the creative will of God is by its nature being-giving. That is to say that the will of God does not keep being for itself alone but truly communicates it (this, and this alone, is the meaning of "to create": to communicate being). Precisely because there is a creation, there are independent entities and things which not only "exist" for themselves, but also, of their own accord, can effect and affect.

This argument was addressed to both opposing sides. The chief objection of the anxious traditionalists in theology was that Thomas allowed creation too great independence of God, and that by defending the rights of natural things he infringed upon the rights of God.[19] To them Thomas cried: The very autonomy and intrinsic effectiveness of created things proves the truly creative powers of God. And to the extremist Aristotelians he said, to set the record straight: You are right; the natural world is a reality in its own right; but there would be no such independent and at the same time nonabsolute reality (for surely you will admit that it is not absolute) if the Creator did not exist.

St. Thomas' second argument runs as follows: Things are good—*all* things. The most compelling proof of their goodness in the very act of being lies in their createdness; there is no more powerful argument for affirmation of the natural reality of the world than the demonstration that the world is *creatura*. Because all things, including the angels, including men, are created, it is for that very reason inconceivable that they themselves should be able to alter essentially their own being or the being of the world; even if they wanted to, they could not destroy being, neither their own nor that of other things. In concrete terms this means: sin, whether on the part of the angels or on the part of men, cannot have essentially changed the structure of the world. Therefore, Thomas argues, I refuse to consider the present state of the world as a basically unnatural state, a state of denaturalization. What is, is good, because it was created by God; whoever casts aspersions upon the perfection of created things casts aspersions upon the perfection of the divine power.[20]

However, there is now a third point to consider. It has been said—and rightly, it seems to me—that Thomas might never have had the courage to defend natural and visible reality, in particular man's corporeality, as an essential part of man, and would never have had the courage to draw the ultimate conclusions from this conviction, had he not thought in terms of the Incarnation of God.[21] The Gospel of John, Thomas says, makes itself so clear on the point that the Logos "became *flesh*," in order to exclude the Manichaean opinion that the body is of evil.[22] One who believes that the Logos of God has, in Christ, united with the bodily nature of man, cannot possibly assume at the same time that the material reality of the world is not good. And how can visible things be evil if the "medicine of Salvation" deriving from that prototypal Sacrament is offered to man in the same visible things, *per ipsa visibilia,* when the Sacraments are performed![23]

Thus the line of reasoning by which Thomas, now appealing strictly to his theological opponents, justified his affirmation of the material world and above all of the human body, was a profoundly theological one. Not only did Thomas justify the right to affirm, but he even insisted on the duty of such affirmation. To sum up, then, Thomas' resolute worldliness set him apart from the spiritualistic, symbolistic unworldliness of the age's traditional theology.

At the same time he differed with the radical, secularistic worldliness of heterodox Aristotelianism by the determinedly theological foundation he gave to his ideas; he justified his worldliness by the theology of creation and by the strictly "theological" theology of the Incarnation.

In the first of these lectures I spoke of how "unharmonious" an era the thirteenth century was, although in terms of the history of thought it might be said that it attained to something like harmony and "classical fullness" for a brief moment. Now it is my opinion that this brief moment was constituted precisely by what I have just been discussing. In this synthesis of a theologically founded worldliness and a theology open to the world, a synthesis Thomas forged with the full energies of his inner being, a culmination was reached. Here was the structure toward which the whole intellectual effort of Christian thinking about the world—from Justin through Augustine and Boethius and Anselm—had been aiming and toward which this whole era of Christendom was directed: the *coniunctio rationis et fidei,* the conjunction of reason with faith. This intellectual structure was, to be sure, not only very highly differentiated; it was also fearfully imperiled and fragile. It had no sooner been erected than it was beset by the forces of disintegration.

I have likewise said earlier that this particular moment has continued to live in the memory of Western Christendom as something exemplary, a paradigm and model, a standard which "really ought" to be met. This is no arbitrary setting up of an ideal. The greatest ideas, those that comprehensively reveal the truth of things, possess some of the obligatory quality of reality itself; they impose an actual coercion. And it can in fact be shown that we—that is to say, Western Christendom and the secular Europeans of the twentieth century who inhabit the soil and live upon the heritage of this Western Christendom—still actually respond to the coercion of that guiding principle which was formulated by Thomas. Thus we simply cannot succeed in living, without uneasiness, in terms of a worldliness wholly divorced from all supramundane calls. It is likewise impossible for us to live, without uneasiness, in terms of a "religionistic" religiousness wholly divorced from all obligations toward the world. We cannot manage, that is, to live consistently against *the* principle which expresses the essence of the Christian West. And the person who for the first time clearly enunciated that principle was none other than Thomas Aquinas.

XI

The guiding principle of a theologically founded worldliness on the one hand and a theology receptive to the world on the other hand established, as I have said, the intellectual structure of the Christian West. There are two further remarks that must be made on this subject. First, that that statement takes cognizance of the fact that a *non-*Western Christianity exists: for example, the Eastern Church, whose theology is emphatically unworldly—though we must also observe that the most thoroughgoing form of principled secularism in history has arisen precisely within the sphere of influence of this form of Christianity.

Non-Western forms of Christianity are, then, conceivable. Nevertheless they remain for us, Western Europeans of the twentieth century, a purely abstract matter. In concrete cases we do not succeed, at any rate not wholly and not consistently, in thinking and living at variance with that Western principle.

Secondly: "The West" is therefore something entirely

different from a specific stock of achievements or institutions. The West is a historical *design,* and one that from the start was laden with explosive potentialities, with the gunpowder of conflict. But, we must realize, this very circumstance—and Thomas obviously had no illusions about it—this very potentiality for conflict, this inescapability of struggles in achieving the design, was accepted and taken into the bargain by all those who affirmed the principle of "theologically founded worldliness." For this principle patently includes the acceptance, for example, of all the findings of natural reason in astronomy, evolution, biology, atomic physics, and science in general. It includes the welcoming of all these findings from the start—in fact, literally, a priori. It includes acceptance of the natural realities of the human condition itself: politics, Eros, technology, and so on. All that, on the one hand; and on the other hand, the principle calls for an allegiance to the standards of a superhuman and supernatural truth with which the temporal truths must be made to square, both on the theoretic plane and in real life.[1]

Now, however, we must speak of a further insight which made St. Thomas' all-embracing reverence for all existing things not only valid, but absolutely compelling and inescapable. It is difficult to say whether the insight in question is a philosophical or a theological one. It concerns the concept of being, or more precisely, the concept of existing. This very phraseology reveals the inherent difficulty of the matter: the peculiarity of existing is just this, that it—existing, existence—cannot be grasped in a "concept."

I should like to try to elucidate my meaning by the use of a thoroughly concrete instance. There before my eyes stands a tree, an oak. Before my eyes—but I also know that many aspects of this tree are not at all visible to the eye, are not accessible to any of the senses. Many aspects of the tree, the essential quality of it, are accessible only to the mind; this essence is only "thinkable," conceivable. I cannot see the vital functioning of the tree as such, not even under the microscope. I now ask about the "essence" of the tree—and this question at first does not involve anything "metaphysical" or philosophical; I am simply seeking an answer to the question: What is a tree? Everyone asks this question, after all, and answers it to his own satisfaction; everyone knows "what" a tree is as distinct from a river, a rock, grass, an animal. Let us assume that it is possible to list every single "quality" of the thing called "tree" and therefore that we can say exhaustively what a tree is—leaving out no characteristic, no conceptual element. Hence, the question, What is a tree? would presumably be answered in full.

Confronted with such an answer, someone might suggest that perhaps the description ought to include a statement as to whether this tree really "exists" or not. At first I would reply that in answering the question, "What is a tree?" the actual existence or nonexistence is of no interest; that I do not look at the matter that way. Whereupon the other may respond that this is precisely what seems to him of crucial importance, that he does not want to know only "what" a tree is, but also whether it really is; he is interested in the *essentia,* the "inwardness," to be sure, but also in the *existentia,* the "thereness." Perhaps we would then consider and discuss this element of "existence." And it will soon turn out that it is not just another conceptual element which can be listed along with the other characteristics—as if we could add to the description of size, shape, kind of foliage, and fruit the additional and final trait of existing. This factor is not co-ordinal with the others; it is something fundamentally different. It has something of the quality of doing. The tree, determined by all those contentual peculiarities, also "does" something: it grows, turns green, bears fruit. And in addition it "does" something else before all these other individual acts: it exists. This act of existing is not only something "of the nature of doing"; it is "doing" in a distinctive and wholly unique sense. The ancients called it "doing" without restriction or further specifications; they simply termed it *actus*.

"The most marvellous of all the things a being can do is: *to be*." In these words Gilson most clearly and convincingly elucidates that insight of St. Thomas which I am discussing here.[2] This, then, is the first matter to be considered: that existence is not one among other substantial characteristics by which an existing thing is determined; existence occupies a position outside this series of characteristics; it is perpendicular to them. Nor is it that a real tree is composed, so to speak, of its essence and its existence; to define the matter thus would be to de-existentialize existence and understand it, or rather misunderstand it, as having to do with the "what is it" of a thing.

But above all, secondly, there is this consideration: in the case of the tree I can in many ways define more closely what "green" means, what "fruitful" or "wood" is, and so on. The substantial characteristics can perhaps not be exhaustively defined, but they can be described and accounted for in greater detail. On the other hand, it is completely impossible to give a more specific explanation of what "existing" means. Anyone who wishes to underline the difference between a real tree and an imaginary one can do no better than to repeat the same phrases: that the real tree exists, that it "actually is," that it is "something real." Existence cannot be defined: *actus . . . definiri non potest*—so says Thomas in his commentary on Aristotle's

Metaphysics.[3] This means that at this point in our considerations—without the slightest exaggeration of the actual facts—our thinking has encountered the riddle of being, perhaps for the first time. Perhaps, to put it more sharply, our thinking meets the *mysterium* of being.

Furthermore (point three): after we have arrived at a relatively adequate answer to the question, "What is a tree?"—by studying and describing really existing trees—we still do not have to make the actual existence of these trees a part of our concept. To exist is not part of their essence; they do not have to exist. There is only One Being of whom it may be said not only that existence is part of His nature, but that His nature consists in existing—so that no appellation more pungently and accurately expresses the nature of this unique Being, namely, God, than the name "He Who Is," the Existing One. "I am Who Am"—so it is put in Holy Scripture (Exodus iii. 14). According to the words of Scripture God Himself calls Himself He Who simply is.

When we innocently hear this phrase, "God is," it at first seems to us that it can be taken to mean only one of two things. Either it is an answer to the question of whether there is a God: "God is," that is to say, God does exist. Or else it is an incomplete sentence, the beginning of a sentence: "God is. . . ." And now the sentence must be rounded out with various statements of what He is: the Creator of all things, merciful, omnipotent, wise . . . and so on. But Thomas takes this phrase neither in the first nor the second meaning, neither as an answer to the question of whether God exists, nor as an incomplete sentence. To his mind the phrase expresses this: God is that Being Whose whole nature it is to exist, that is to say, to be the *actus*. God is existence in itself, *actus purus*. Where God is concerned, it is not possible to say, or even merely to

137

think, that a certain being exists, determined by a certain sum of characteristics, and that in addition there is—perhaps necessarily—His existence, the actuality of this being whose nature is such and such. No, if we wish to speak in the most precise possible terms, without being figurative, without bending our language to meet the ordinary needs of conversation, then we must say: God's essential nature itself is actuality; He *is* His actuality. *In Deo non est aliud essentia vel quidditas quam suum esse;* in God essence and existence are not twain.[4]

To say this is to make a "revolution" in the history of metaphysics; and the revolutionary was Thomas.[5] However, this revolution became possible only as the result of further developing the Aristotelian distinction between potential being and actual being, between *dynamis* and *enérgeia*.[6] Perhaps we must also say that it was made possible by an intellectual link between the Aristotelian concept of *enérgeia* and the Biblical name of God, "I am Who Am." Gilson has pointed out that another great philosopher-theologian who endeavored to think Aristotle through, and to integrate the problems posed by Aristotle with a theology based on revelation, namely, the Jewish genius Moses Maimonides, had formulated this concept of being and of God almost one hundred years before the time of Thomas, and for the first time.[7] Thomas, however —Gilson continues—was the first to pursue this path consistently and to the end.

No such interpretation of the concept of Being could conceivably have arisen out of Platonic thinking; Plato and his followers had been fascinated, in their philosophizing, by the idea of archetypes, that is to say, of pure essences remote from all existential realization. In specifically historical terms this meant that Christian philosophy and theology before Thomas Aquinas was simply incapable of conceiving of Being in this existential manner. Étienne

Gilson, Jacques Maritain, and other French scholars have expressly termed St. Thomas' metaphysics an "existential philosophy." "I am convinced that Thomas is the most existential of the philosophers," *le plus existentiel des philosophes*.[8] "As philosophy of the act-of-being Thomism is not *another* existential philosophy, it is the only one."[9] Above all, says Gilson, Augustine's and Anselm's thinking about the problem of Being was, in comparison with Thomas', completely "essentialistic."[10]

In his exegesis of the Gospel of John, Augustine asks himself the meaning of the divine name, "I am Who Am." We might also put it: he faces up to this question; for Augustine recognized very well the weight and the mystery implicit in those words. "The Lord then said to Moses: *I am Who Am. . . .* He did not say: *I am God,* or *I am the Author of the world,* or *I am the Creator of all things,* or *I am the guardian of this people who must be liberated.* Rather, he said only this: *I am Who Am!* But O Lord, our God, what then *is not* of all that You have created? *Is* the sky not? *Is* the earth not also? And the man to whom you speak, *is* he not? Must we then understand this *I am Who Am* as if everything else *were* not?" Whereupon Augustine answers himself, speaking in the manner of prayer: "Let then Being itself, the *ipsum esse,* say what it is; let it say this to the heart. . . . Let the inner man, let his thinking mind understand that 'truly to be' means: to be always in the same way"; *vere esse est enim semper eodem modo esse.*[11]

In his maturest and most speculative work, the books on the Trinity, Augustine summed the matter up once more: "Perhaps it should be said that God alone is *essentia*. For he alone truly is because he is immutable—and it is this he declared to Moses, his servant, when he declared: 'I am Who Am.' "[12] This is a clearly "essentialistic" interpretation of the concept of Being; Being at its most intense is to be found in immutable essence. The concepts of reality found in Boethius, Anselm, and Bonaventura spring from this same basic idea of Augustine. And then along comes Thomas and says: "I am Who Am" means: I am He Whose essence it is to exist. When Augustine read the divine name he understood it to mean: "I am He Who never changes." When Thomas read the same words he understood them to say: "I am the pure act-of-being."[13]

I have said that this insight of St. Thomas, this particular view of the concept of Being and of God, made affirmation of everything that is inevitable and compelling to him. In order to see why this is so, we must do a bit of reasoning. First: What makes things truly "real" is the act of existing. That is, the substantial fullness of being is not primarily decisive; what is decisive is the simple but unfathomable fact which distinguishes a possible human being from an actual human being. Naturally there is a hierarchy of existing beings according to the substantial richness of the being, according to the perfection of the *essentia*. But the question must first be asked: What is the meaning of "greater fullness of being"? Could it not consist in deeper intensity of existing? But first and foremost the step from nonexistence to actual existence is incomparably more crucial than the step from plant to animal or from animal to man. The crucial factor is *the "actus,"* doing as such, the actual realization of the state of being: *esse est illud quod est intimum cuilibet et quod profundius omnibus inest,* to be, the act-of-being, is the innermost thing for every being and that which is most deeply of all embodied in each.[14]

Secondly: None of the beings we are acquainted with can bring about this *actus,* this simple state of being, of its own accord. Above all we ourselves—that is perfectly obvious to everyone—are absolutely incapable of making something existent out of something nonexistent. Nothing of the sort has ever been done, and there is every indication that it cannot ever be done. Nothing is more undeniable than this. We can, to be sure, make something out of something that already exists; but we cannot make this or any other something exist. We cannot create anything.

If, on the other hand, creating means bringing things forth into being, *productio rerum in esse,* then creation is above all bringing into existence. Augustine, in explaining the concept of *creatio,* declares that it is the act by which He Who is what He is makes things be what they are: stone, tree, animal, man, angel. Gilson has remarked that "one of the first consequences of this doctrine is to de-existentialize completely the notion of creation."[15] Thomas, on the other hand, had already formulated his answer to this problem in his first book, *De ente et essentia.* (And these latest considerations of ours throw an entirely new light upon the fact that the young man of twenty-seven instantly came to grips with this most sublime of all metaphysical problems.) In the very first chapter of this early *opusculum* Thomas says: *essentia* means that the thing which is in it has *existence.*[16] Things are not truly and ultimately "in existence" by *what* they are, but by the *actus essendi.* And this, the communication of the *actus essendi,* that is to say, of sheer existence—precisely this is creation in the full sense of the word: *Primus effectus Dei in rebus est ipsum esse, quod omnes alii effectus praesupponunt,* "the first fruit of God's activity in things is existence itself; all other effects presuppose it—existence."[17] And here are two more sentences from the *Summa theologica's* doctrine of the Creation: "Because God by virtue of His essence is existence itself, therefore the existence of what he has created is necessarily a producing peculiar to His essence; just as flaming up is the effect peculiar to the essence of fire."[18] And: *"Therefore* God must be *in* all things, and in the most intimate manner"; *oportet quod Deus sit in omnibus rebus et intime.*[19]

Reduced to the briefest formula, the sum total of all this amounts to the following: Wherever we encounter anything real, anything existent in any way whatsoever, we encounter something that has "flamed up" directly from God. We are dealing with something that is similar to the Existent-in-itself—and not on the basis of an "added" perfection, but on the basis of existence itself: *in quantum habet esse, est Ei simile.*[20]

Platonic thinking makes much of the conception of an ascent to God by way of the hierarchic ladder of essences, of a gradual approximation to the immutable Being of God. Thomas, on the other hand, says: Every existing thing—whether alive or not, whether material or spiritual, whether perfected or wretched, and in fact whether good or evil—everything that has existence, confronts us in the most direct way with the primal reality of God. If we regard what exists, whatever it may be, *as* something existent ("of course we cannot see existence, but we know it is there and we can at least locate it, by an act of judgment, as the hidden root of what we can see and of what we can attempt to define"[21])—if we determinedly seek to fathom what it is that "acts" before our eyes, which can see a grain of matter, a birch twig, or a human countenance, then the thought is inevitably borne upon us: this is something that has flamed up out of the *actus purus.* And therefore, strictly speaking, it is too little to say: everything that is, is good because it is; "for every thing, to be and to be good, is the same," *idem est unicuique rei esse et bonum esse.*[22] This, in fact, falls short of the total affirmation which flows out of the concept of being formulated by Thomas. Rather, it should be put this way: because the being of the world participates in the divine being which pervades it to its innermost core, the world is not only a good world; it is in a very precise sense *holy*.[23]

It would lead us too far afield to attempt to show in detail that this statement by no means draws all the sting from reality. I have said: we cannot make anything exist. But beings to whom freedom has been given can intensify their own existence by their affirmation as well as weaken it by their negation. We can, on the basis of our own freedom, even resist the complete actualization of ourselves. Precisely this is the concept of evil; understood in these terms, evil, like the concept of existence itself, likewise possesses "absolute" character. If existing is not only good but also holy, then the rejection of existence is not only evil but also sacrilegious, anti-godly.

This is the point at which to pose a new and extremely basic question: whether all this has not long since drifted off—if it were there from the very start—into the realm of *theology;* whether this sort of thing has not ceased to be philosophy or even metaphysics. This question reaches far beyond the subject last discussed. It concerns the whole Thomas. It also concerns what we ourselves are engaged in here. In what sense are these lectures in philosophy?

Thomas was obviously both philosopher and theologian. An explicitly theological lecture on St. Thomas would discuss quite other matters, with which we have not formally dealt here: the doctrine of the Trinity, the doctrine of the Incarnation, the Sacraments. The question is whether we can wholly isolate the theological from the philosophical elements in the works of Thomas, and can consider the one apart from the other. Gilson says that the theology of St. Thomas is a philosopher's theology and his philosophy is a theologian's.[24]

I propose to attack this problem in the following manner: To consider the question whether theology can exist at all, and what it is, and how theology relates to, say, the sciences and to philosophy—such considerations are, at any rate, not yet theology. These are themes, we say, for a philosophical theory of knowledge. And we now have to see what Thomas thought of the relationship of theology and philosophy. If it is true that Thomas attacked the task of reconciling "Aristotle" and the "Bible" with the utmost critical reflectiveness, well knowing what he was undertaking, then he was also undertaking to clarify the relationship between theology and philosophy.

To regard fire as fire is philosophy; to regard fire not as itself but as a symbol of the divine life is theology— I have already cited this statement from the *Summa Against the Pagans,* not so much to show what Thomas meant by theology as to show what he meant by philosophy. These words do not yet pinpoint what theology really is. "Not yet"—that is something we can rarely say of Thomas; for we are forever astonished by the sureness with which, at his first attack, he can go to the heart of a matter.[25] What he says concerning theology in the above statement is an accurate rendering of the viewpoint widely held in his day: that theology was reality in symbolic guise. But this particular definition of theology is found, it appears, only in Thomas' early writings, in the *Commentary on the Sentences*[26] or in the *Summa Against the Pagans.*[27] Later, he expresses himself differently. But is not theology simply the "doctrine of God?" No, that is not its decisive feature, Thomas says; there is a doctrine of God which is not at all theology, but philosophy.[28]

Theology in the strict sense is, in its logical structure, something far more "derivative," more complicated, and more difficult than philosophy. To philosophize means to direct our gaze into the world and at ourselves and, thus holding our eyes fixed upon reality, to ask about the ultimate meaning of the whole which embraces the universe and man and God (insofar as God appears before our gaze in our contemplation of the world, or in our inner experience—within our own consciences, say). But to pursue theology is something else again. Theology does not presuppose only the appearance of a world before our eyes, and behind it, deducible or intuitable, God, while we ourselves stand confronting this objective reality, experiencing, thinking, questioning. No, theology assumes more than this, and different things. Theology exists only on the basis of the fact that men have received certain tidings out of the sphere of the supramundane God, a message which is not already contained in the world itself, which cannot be read by querying reality and listening to its answers. What is meant by these "tidings" is that God has spoken anew and unforeseeably, and in a manner audible to man. Theology, then, exists only if revelation exists. That is one prerequisite of theology, and the most important. The second prerequisite is that man not only hears these tidings, but also accepts them—that is, that he believes. Theology, then, is the effort by the believer and for the believer to reach an interpretation of revelation; it is the attempt to understand as fully as possible the audible speech of God contained in the documents of revelation. Theology is *doctrina secundum revelationem divinam,* says Thomas in the first *articulus* of the *Summa theologica.*[29] *Sacra doctrina considerat aliqua secundum quod sunt divinitus revelata.*[30]

Without revelation, then, and without its being accepted with faith, theology is not possible. But given those prerequisites, theology is possible and as a rule comes into being. This statement may sound theoretic, but its connotations are concrete, even forcefully so, and have a direct bearing on the practitioner of philosophy. Plato undoubtedly understood the sacred tradition of the myths as lore descended from a divine source,[31] that is to say, as revelation; and he believed this lore ("You think it a story, I think it truth"[32]). From which it follows that the effort undertaken in the Platonic dialogues to extract the true meaning from the symbolic language of the myths is theology in the strict sense of the word.

Now the truly exciting thing is that Thomas, too, would term this Platonic interpretation of the myths theology in the strict sense. For he, along with most theologians of the Christian West, was ready to allow that revelation, the veritable speech of God, had been vouchsafed to men outside Holy Scripture. *Multis gentilium facta fuit revelatio;* "revelation has been made to many pagans"—this was an opinion that Thomas pronounced many times.[33] In line with this, he saw no difficulty in assuming that the Sibyls, say, had spoken under an *inspiratio divina.* There is no need for us to compile further instances. But it is important for us to grasp the full implications of this concept of "God's speech" sounding and resounding throughout the mythical tradition of many nations.[34] It means that theology as the interpretation of that divine speech (about the meaning of the universe and about human salvation) is a perfectly self-evident matter spread over the whole breadth of man's mental life!

Before we go more deeply into the relationship of theology and philosophy which is founded in the nature of both, we must first issue this warning: There is not the slightest sense in anyone's investigating this question who does not accept the existence of theology at all; that is to say, someone who neither acknowledges the fact of revelation nor accepts the content of revelation as the truth. I say that without this prerequisite any investigation of the relationship between philosophy and theology remains a purely hypothetical and abstract business. Indeed, I go further; I venture to assert that this investigation is not even possible as an intellectual "sport." Certain things cannot be undertaken sportively—not so much because to do so is improper as because it will not work, it simply cannot be done. Thus, it is simply not possible to say: Let us assume that the Christians are right and let us see where this assumption carries us. For one can only "see" it, that is, one catches sight of the light that falls from the truth of religion upon reality, only if one identifies oneself existentially with what is believed. The question, then, of how theology and philosophy may be related in their essences to one another—both being taken as vital acts of the mind—can be meaningfully investigated only if both acts are actually carried out.

Most discussions on this subject are sham discussions. In reality they deal with an entirely different subject, namely, whether theology is possible at all, whether anything like revelation exists and, if so, how do we recognize it, what grounds are there for faith—and so on. These subjects are, of course, extremely important; they are absolutely fundamental; it is essential that they be discussed. But they are *different* subjects; they have nothing to do with the question of the mutual relationship of theology and philosophy.

XII

To philosophize means, we have said, to concentrate our gaze upon the totality of encountered phenomena and methodically to investigate the coherency of them all and the ultimate meaning of the Whole; to examine what "something real" actually is, what man himself is, mind, the complete total of things. To pursue theology means endeavoring to discover what really was said in the divine revelation.

If we direct our gaze not so much upon the structure of these two acts as upon their object, that is to say, upon the thing that the two acts deal with, we will first of all note the following: The philosophical act deals, by definition, with everything that is—insofar as what is can be seen by a gaze directed at the encountered phenomena.[1] The philosophical thinker observes reality, whatever it may be. And he observes things as themselves, fire as fire, and so on. The practitioner of theology, on the other hand, deals with the utterances of the *theios logos;* he deals with all those things with which divine revelation is concerned. But with what is revelation concerned?

This much is clear at once: to one who is engaged in theology it is impossible to delimit a specific realm of subject matter. For that would mean presuming to limit the speech of God to specific subjects. We need only express this to expose the absurdity of any such undertaking: it is obviously not for us to determine what God may speak of and what not. This means that it is likewise impossible to say that theology ought to deal with those things that lie beyond the range of natural knowledge. The documents of revelation contain many things that "in themselves" are also comprehensible to the natural cognitive powers of man and attainable by those powers. Thomas went out of his way to show the significance of that.[2]

But what in fact is the content of revelation? If we were to pose this question to Plato, we would receive an answer along the following lines: Sacred tradition declares that the world emerged from the unenvying goodness of its Founder;[3] that God holds in His hands the beginning, the middle, and the end of all things;[4] that the spirit holds dominion over the Whole of the universe;[5] that after death the good may expect something far better than the bad;[6] that the soul is imperishable[7]—and so on. The astonishing thing is that these propositions of Plato are in fundamental agreement with certain propositions of Christian revelation, although in a way all their own. The common theme is the divine guarantee of the world and of human salvation. But this means that theology likewise has to deal with the world as a whole, and above all with human existence as a whole.

Both the philosopher and the theologian, therefore, seek to discover how the world as a whole is constituted and, above all, what man's ultimate situation is. It is this universality of their questions which marks off both philosophy and theology from all other disciplines. Every other discipline establishes itself by adopting a selective viewpoint; no other discipline asks about the universe as a whole. Philosophy and theology are different. They can afford to ignore the problem of purity and untaintedness of method. To put this negatively, the problem of overstepping limits—that is, the given frontiers of a discipline—is virtually meaningless for both philosophy and theology; it is almost nonexistent.

The philosopher, then, is not really characterized by the practice of a specific discipline of clearly delineated methods. We might almost say that the person seriously engaged in philosophizing is not at all interested in "philosophy." He wants to know how the universe and man as a whole are constituted—but, to be sure, *insofar* as these can be seen by a completely open and unprejudiced gaze directed at the encountered phenomena. What is the meaning of "can be seen"? If something that we cannot actually discern nevertheless is forced upon us as an unavoidable conclusion; if in encountered phenomena themselves something is suggested to us, something we can guess at or possibly intuit—is this something that "can be seen"? At any rate, insofar as we philosophize when we look upon man we become "unphilosophical" if we say that since we are investigating the "metaphysical essence of man" we cannot be bothered by what biology, psychology, or the general science of human behavior has to say about him. Nor is this the only manner in which we can sin against philosophy. We are also sinning against it if we say we are not interested in the assertion of theologians that some grave misfortune fraught with consequences for all time to come happened to man in primordial times. Plato, at any rate, thought the question worth his while when he examined the ultimate nature of Eros in the *Symposium;* he gave close attention to the myth of primordial man's fall. *Apud philosophos,* says Thomas, *Philosophia Prima utitur omnium scientiarum documentis;* the *philosophia prima,* the most philosophical philosophy, makes use of the findings of all the sciences.[8]

The theologian proceeds in very similar fashion, casting his line far beyond the borders of a methodologically delimited special discipline. In order to carry out his specifically theological task—disclosing the real meaning of divine utterance—the theologian may not confine himself to what we may call a purely "Biblicistic" approach to revelation. Rather, keeping his eye fixed upon his own goal, he must additionally take into consideration everything else that he knows about the subject under discussion, no matter what its source. How, for example, in interpreting the Biblical account of Creation, could he studiously ignore all that evolutionary research, paleontology, or biology has already uncovered, or is still bringing to light? In practicing his own profession, then, the theologian's first concern is not with "methodologically pure" theology—although that is also one of his themes. Far more important questions confront him. Thus, for example, he may try to explain what is meant by the sentence: "God formed man of dust from the ground, and breathed into his nostrils the breath of life," taking into account all we know of geology, of man as a living being, and of man's prehistory. Thomas seems to have anticipated this task, for in Thomas we may read: "The knowledge of religion presupposes natural knowledge";[9] "evidently those who teach Holy Scripture [that is, the theologians] must also make use of worldly wisdom";[10] "errors about Creation occasionally lead men astray from the truth of faith too."[11]

In sum, neither the philosopher nor the theologian can presume to exclude any available information on the subject at hand. The moment there is such an exclusion, philosophy or theology is not truly being practiced. Naturally it is unrealistic to demand that the philosopher and the theologian explicitly include, or in fact even be informed, about all that there is to be known. On the other hand, this is precisely why both philosophy and theology are fundamentally "impossible." Dilthey has described the task of the philosopher thus: "The demands upon the person engaged in philosophizing cannot be met. A physicist is a pleasant reality, useful to himself and others; the philosopher, like the saint, exists only as an ideal."[12]

Taking this proposition as our starting point, let us consider the question of the mutual co-ordination of philosophy and theology. For the theologian the question runs this way: If one is convinced that God has spoken, and seeks to determine what a particular teaching of revelation means, taking into consideration everything he already knows and everything that is revealed elsewhere—what does philosophy mean to such a person and his endeavors? By philosophy, of course, we do not mean any given set of theses and arguments propounded by a philosopher, but rather the philosophical act itself.

And for the philosopher the question runs this way: If

one who fixes his gaze upon the world and himself should ask the ultimate meaning of the encountered phenomena, what does theology—that is, the interpretation of the divine speech—mean to him? What value can he find in it, when to the believer in its truth this divine speech so piercingly illuminates reality? What part does this coordinate relationship play in, say, Thomas' "existential" interpretation of the concept of Being? "Is it St. Thomas the theologian who, reading in Exodus the identity of essence and existence in God, taught St. Thomas the philosopher the distinction between essence and existence in creatures? Or is it St. Thomas the philosopher who, pushing his analysis of the metaphysical structure of the concrete even as far as the distinction between essence and existence, taught St. Thomas the theologian that *He Who Is* in Exodus means the *Act-of-Being?*"[13]

If Thomas' theological interpretation of this divine name is a whole dimension deeper than St. Augustine's interpretation, is Thomas indebted to philosophy (or even to Aristotle)? Or is it the philosophical conception of Being which here profits by the experience of theology? Must we not say that what takes place is a unitary act, or a compound of acts which is no longer separable into its philosophical and theological "components"? Of course the philosophical element can still be distinguished theoretically from the theological element. But concretely the situation in that a living man, confronted with the Whole of reality—one Thomas Aquinas—as believer and thinker (and experiencer of sense perceptions), as a man reflecting upon his beliefs and at the same time observing man and the universe with all his powers of natural cognition, asks himself: What is all this about? We cannot extract a system of philosophy out of the works of St. Thomas and present it in isolation, for itself; if we did that, the result would be, as Gilson says, rather a philosophy *"ad mentem Cartesii"* than one *"ad mentem sancti Thomae."*[14]

To be sure, Thomas himself made a point of distinguishing between philosophy and theology. But he made the distinction in order to join, not to part. By their nature philosophy and theology belong together in a unity of form. To be sure, this unity is achieved only in the living thought of the philosopher who believes in the divine revelation and undertakes, in his reflections, to consider and to comprehend the revealed material (which, as a questioner investigating the coherency of the Whole, the philosopher cannot omit to do); and only in the living thought of the theologian who is convinced that man's natural powers of cognition are also capable of truly grasping reality, and who likewise cannot omit considering all available information on the universe and man.

Anyone who accepts this line of reasoning must see at once how dubious an affair is the dispute and the indignation which are generally kindled by the proposition that philosophy is the "handmaiden" of theology, the *ancilla theologiae.* This argument has long since ceased to be even dubious; it has simply become boring.

Historically, the phrase "handmaiden of theology" appears to have been employed for the first time by the Jewish religious philosopher Philo (died circa A.D. 50). Among the Fathers of the Church similar terms are quite common.[15]

Far more interesting is the circumstance that Thomas is representing two sources which mingle when he speaks of this matter. And these two sources are, once again, Aristotle and the Bible. Aristotle asks, at the beginning of his *Metaphysics,* What are the characteristics which everyone attributes to real, true wisdom?[16] And discussing this matter, he makes the point that wisdom is a governing, not a servile principle. The wise man does not serve, but is served; *sapientum . . . non decet ordinari ab alio, sed ipsum potius alios ordinare*—thus Thomas in his commentary on the passage.[17] Thomas then takes occasion to mention the other source, Holy Scripture: "[Divine] wisdom sends out her handmaidens to invite men to her castle" (Prov. ix. 3).[18]

But, of course, those who are concerned for philosophy's independence of theology are not entirely in the wrong. Philosophy does not "serve" for anything, because it is concerned with wisdom. This is just what distinguishes philosophy from the separate sciences. It is not "subordinate" to any adventitious purpose. No one has ever waxed indignant because medical science is obviously the "handmaiden" of practical healing and is constantly receiving orders and suggestions from the practitioners of medicine. Everyone takes it for granted that physics and chemistry are fields of practical endeavor serving technological, economic, or military ends. The distinctive feature of philosophy is that by its nature it cannot be taken into service in any such fashion. Does that mean that its services may also not be enlisted by theology?

I would answer this tricky question as follows: Theology's way of "enlisting the services" of philosophy is something quite different. In its very essence, this process is different from and not to be compared with the way practicality draws upon the services of the sciences. Philosophizing aims at wisdom, we have said, and moreover, at wisdom for its own sake. But theology, which comes forward with claims to "dominance," is a higher form of wisdom itself! To enlist philosophy in the services of theology, then, does not mean to subordinate it to any alien, adventitious end. Rather, the end inherent in the act of philosophizing itself—namely, wisdom itself, "knowledge of the highest causes"—is the very same goal that is attainable and achievable in religion and in theology on a higher plane than in philosophy. Naturally, this argument will appeal only to one who has already accepted theology itself as a meaningful thing; and indeed, the whole problem of the co-ordination of philosophy and theology exists for him alone. But for him it is a clear self-evident axiom that what all philosophizing truly seeks is divine wisdom, and that God's speech stands higher than human speech.

Unfortunately, however, the matter is still somewhat more complicated. For after all theology is not simply identical with "God's speech" and "divine wisdom." Theology involves *human* speech; it involves the human effort to interpret revelation. And understood in these terms, theology naturally stands within the fully charged field of human existence—with all its possible contingencies, including that of degeneration. It is, for example, eminently conceivable that theology may misunderstand its relationship to philosophy and come forth with a wrongful claim to dominance. And this is not just "conceivable." In fact, Thomas had to defend the independence of philosophy against such overweening claims by the theology of his times. For other theologians of his time—and the tendency is an eternal one—held that the subjects of philosophy should be limited to theologically important matters, to the things theology needed; or at least the theologian must limit his own incursions into philosophy to such subjects. That was, for example, the opinion which Bonaventura set forth in his famous essay, *De reductione artium ad theologiam*.[19] Thomas was directly opposed to this, and not only in the name of philosophy, but also in the name of theology itself, which needed the link with a free and independent philosophy.

St. Thomas' thesis, as it is expressed in his actual procedure, can be formulated approximately as follows: First, on the basis of the mere definition of theology and philosophy no theologian can say in advance what philosophical insights, or in general what natural insights, are or may be of importance to him. It may be that the theologian "needs" *everything,* just as, on the other hand, each error concerning the universe or man may possibly become a stumbling block to him, or even fatally undermine his work.[20] Therefore, as Thomas says, it is praiseworthy to study the secular sciences for their own sake.[21] In this connection he quotes St. Jerome who speaks of *sancta rusticitas,* of sacred ignorance, which is at most useful to itself.[22]

Second: The theologian too, in spite of revelation, is dealing with a hidden, by no means obvious truth into which he must probe ever more deeply.[23] But no one can state beforehand the manner or the direction in which he ought to probe. The clue may well come to light only on the basis of certain philosophical or scientific insights which could never have been foreseen by theologians; which, in fact, would be unwelcome to theologians because of the inevitable uneasiness they engender. Theology is a human enterprise and therefore shares the limits, the possibilities of degeneracy, and therefore the need for correction inherent in all things human—and does so in a specific manner corresponding to its nature.

Yes, theology has its own failings. On this subject we are indebted to the realistic viewpoint of the Anglo-Saxon mind for a number of remarks, as aggressive as they are sound, which are wholly within the spirit of St. Thomas. We are thinking of certain things said by John Henry Newman and Friedrich von Huegel. Newman has observed that the typical degenerative symptoms of theology are "systematization, phantasticality, dogmatism and bigotry." By *bigotry* he means a kind of self-imposed limitation of religion to itself, a fearful shutting itself away from the fresh wind of experience and knowledge of reality. By this, he says, theology itself corrupts its best and most intrinsic potentialities; and the ultimate result is sectarianism, sophistry, and tale-bearing.[24]

Friedrich von Huegel, one of the greatest intellects of modern Christendom, has said time and again that theology, for the sake of its own health, needs the resistance of science and philosophy; that theology must brave "this savage current." "All genuine mystics have a sort of aura which shows that they really passed through fire and water. Nicholas of Cues, Pascal, and Malebranche are only three among many for whom mysticism and mathematico-physical science mutually stimulated one another and together gave the soul its depth."[25]

In St. Thomas' opinion theology is, to be sure, the higher form of wisdom, being the interpretation of revelation. But in order to practice its own trade it needs the tools of science and philosophy. *Propter defectum intellectus nostri,* because of the failings of our own intellect—and the theologian must also fall back upon human intellect when he engages in theology—because of this weakness, theology requires the independently obtained information of natural knowledge; theology "makes use" of it, "presupposes it,"[26] listens to it, takes note of it, and learns from it. Seen in this light, does not this somewhat tasteless business of asking which "serves" what become meaningless?

It may, then, be said with complete accuracy that this formal unity of philosophy and theology is the structural principle of St. Thomas' *summas,* especially his *Summa theologica.* But we must quickly interpose a word, to avert an almost inevitable misunderstanding. It is the misunderstanding of assuming that the *summas* are the most pretentious form of closed system—the closed system in the sense of Hegel, who says: "The true form in which truth exists can only be the scientific system of truth."[27] By this misunderstanding, the *Summa theologica* would pretend to be a system in which every question is treated and answered in its place, an adequate reflection of the essential reality of the universe—a total solution wherein even those problems which natural reason alone cannot settle would be given their final clarification in the answers of faith and theology.

We must first consider the purely external fact that St. Thomas' *Summa theologica* remained unfinished. Incidentally, it is not quite proper to call this an "external fact." For it was not that early death snatched the pen from St. Thomas' hand. This point is apt to be misrepresented in the notes to be found in various editions of the *Summa*. The real story is this: that on a precisely noted day, December 6, 1273, returning to his cell from the celebration of Mass, Thomas declared that writing had become repugnant to him. "All that I have written seems to me nothing but straw—compared with what I have seen and what has been revealed to me." And he abided by this decision. This means that the fragmentary character of the *Summa theologica* is an inherent part of its statement.

That act of falling silent, however, was only the most superficial existential embodiment of an attitude which Thomas had already expounded, and whose theoretical basis he made clearer and clearer with the passing of the years. This attitude is revealed not only in the fragmentary character of the work; not only in what is missing, but also in what he explicitly says. For he explicitly says that all our knowledge, including the knowledge of theologians, is fragmentary in character. The clarity of St. Thomas' diction is deceptive. Chenu speaks of argumentation "within the mystery."[28] Thomas was so little a classicist of systematic thought that, on the contrary, we become aware that he cherished "an extreme suspicion of systems," *une extrème défiance des systèmes*.[29]

If we cannot make Thomas into a "classicist," we certainly cannot make him an advocate of any "ism." If "Thomists" claim that they can reduce the doctrine of St. Thomas to a system of propositions that can be transmitted by the tradition of a school, then their "Thomism" must be called a falsification. For they will have suppressed the very feature in which, so it seems to me, lies the greatness of St. Thomas as a philosophical and theological thinker: his attitude of veneration toward everything that is—which veneration is revealed above all in his falling silent before the ineffability and incomprehensibility of Being. Thomas goes even further than to say, as he does in a manner which is most unsettling, that we do not know what God is. This statement may be found at the very beginning of the *Summa theologica*, where it may be read by all, even by the rankest of "beginners": *De Deo scire non possumus quid sit, sed quid non sit;* "We cannot know what God is, but rather only what He is not."[30] What is more, Thomas elaborates on this matter, and actually calls ignorance the best part of knowledge itself: "This is the extreme of human knowledge of God: to know that we do not know God," *quod homo sciat se Deum nescire*.[31]

But, as I have said, Thomas goes even further, for he not only asserts that we cannot know the nature of God, but also that we are incapable of getting to the bottom of created things—and for the reason that things, all things aside from God, are creature. To be creature means, in the first place: to be the image of a divine design, a design that is necessarily inaccessible to us. And to be creature means, in the second place: as an existent thing to have flamed up by the *actus purus;* but since existence itself is so incomprehensible, we cannot even properly say it "exists." "Just as we cannot say that *running* itself *runs,* so we also cannot say that *being* itself *is, quod ipsum esse sit.*"[32]

Once we have been alerted to this motif, we will see how central it is to the thinking of Thomas. Again and again we will encounter sentences for which the "Thomism" of the schools has not prepared us, and which in fact burst the bounds of every "system"—such as, for example, the sentence: *Rerum essentiae sunt nobis ignotae:* "The essence of things is unknown to us."[33]

All this has nothing whatsoever to do with "agnosticism." St. Thomas does not hold the thesis that neither God nor things are knowable. On the contrary, they are so utterly knowable that we can never come to the end of our endeavors to know them. It is precisely their knowability that is inexhaustible.[34] This means in the first place that we must be extremely wary whenever someone comes forward with a claim to have found the ultimate formula for the universe; it means that we must be on guard against every sort of "ism," be it existentialism or Marxism or even Thomism. But guardedness and wariness are only one side of the coin, only half the conclusion to be drawn from the thesis that things are simultaneously knowable and incomprehensible. The other side is an intrepid frankness of affirmation, an enthusiasm for ever new explorations into the wonders of reality. Along with that, of course, there come ever new difficulties in incorporating the new data into our total view of the universe, and hence ever new conflicts, compelling us constantly to rethink our previous positions, to revise all our set ideas, even in theology. This attitude, which neither permits us to cast away an insight already won nor allows us to rest on our laurels with a false sense of finality, is not easy to achieve. It is a highly demanding affair. But it is perhaps the best lesson among the many that can be learned in the school of the "universal teacher" of Christendom.

The quotations from the *Summa theologica* are identified in the following notes only by numerals. For example, II, II, 123, 2 ad 4 means: Second Part of the Second Part, quaestio 123, articulus 2, reply to Objection 4. The same code is used for references to the commentary on the *Sentences* of Peter Lombard. For example, 3, d, 31, 2, 5 means: Book Three, distinctio 31, quaestio 2, articulus 5. The titles of the other works of St. Thomas cited in the text are abbreviated as follows:

C. G.	*Summa Against the Pagans* (*Summa contra Gentiles*)
Ver.	*Quaestiones disputatae de veritate*
Mal.	*Quaestiones disputatae de malo*
Pot.	*Quaestiones disputatae de potentia Dei*
Spir. creat.	*Quaestio disputata de spiritualibus creaturis*
Quol.	*Quaestiones quodlibetales*
Substant. separ.	*De substantiis separatis*
Un. int.	*De unitate intellectus contra Averroistas*
Reg. princ.	*On the Governance of Princes*
Comp. theol.	*Compendium theologiae*
Perf. vit. spir.	*De perfectione vitae spiritualis*
Contra impugn.	*Contra impugnantes Dei cultum et religionem*
Contra retrah.	*Contra retrahentes homines a religionis ingressu*
In John.	Commentary on the Gospel of John
In Met.	Commentary on Aristotle's *Metaphysics*
In An.	Commentary on Aristotle's *On the Soul*
In Phys.	Commentary on Aristotle's *Physics*
Contra err. Graec.	*Against the Errors of the Greeks*
In De caelo et mundo	Commentary on Aristotle's *On the Heavens*

In Trin.	Commentary on Boethius' *On the Trinity*
In Hebd.	Commentary on Boethius' *Essay on Axioms* (*De hebdomadibus*)
Virt. card.	*Quaestio disputata de virtutibus cardinalibus*

NOTES

I

[1] Fernand van Steenberghen, *Le XIIIe siècle*. In Forest, van Steenberghen, and de Gandillac, *Le Mouvement doctrinal du XIe au XIVe siècle*. Fliche-Martin, *Histoire de l'Église,* vol. 13 (Paris, 1951), p. 303.

[2] Étienne Gilson, *History of Christian Philosophy in the Middle Ages* (London and New York, 1955), p. 325.

[3] Friedrich Heer, *Europäische Geistesgeschichte* (Stuttgart, 1953), p. 147.

[4] Marie-Dominique Chenu, *Introduction à l'étude de St. Thomas d'Aquin* (Paris–Montreal, 1950), p. 13.

[5] Gustav Schnürer, *Kirche und Kultur im Mittelalter* (Paderborn, 1926), II, p. 441.

[6] *Liber primus Posteriorum Analyticorum,* tract. 1, cap. 1 *Opera Omnia.* Ed. A. Borgnet (Paris, 1890), tom. 2, p. 3.

[7] C. G. 1, 2.

[8] Gilson, *History,* p. 325.

[9] Joseph Lortz, *Die Reformation in Deutschland* (Freiburg im Breisgau, 1939), I, p. 352.

[10] Heidelberg, 1956.

[11] Maisie Ward, *Gilbert Keith Chesterton* (New York, 1943), p. 620.

[12] The latest (eighth) edition was published in 1949 by Kösel Verlag, Munich.

[13] Paris, 1950.

[14] The fifth French edition was published in Paris in 1948; the

English edition, from which we quote in the following pages, appeared in 1957 in London.

[15] Cf. "Les poésies de Rinaldo d'Aquino" (ed. O. Tallgren), in *Mémoires de la Société Néophilologique de Helsingfors,* vol. 6 (1917).

[16] Contra retrah. 9; No. 803.

[17] Martin Grabmann, *Mittelalterliches Geistesleben* (Munich, 1926), I, p. 261.

[18] Reg. princ. 1, 8–10.

II

[1] Martin Grabmann, "Die Kanonisation des heiligen Thomas." *Divus Thomas,* Jahrgang 1 (1923), pp. 241 f.

[2] Contra impugn. 1, 1; No. 11.

[3] *Vita S. Thomae* 6, 31. Ed. D. Prümmer (St. Maximin, 1924).

[4] *Oratio ad vitam sapienter instituendam. Opuscula Theologica.* Ed. R. M. Spiazzi (Turin–Rome, 1954), vol. 2, p. 285.

[5] Thus the Thomas encyclical of Pius XI, "Studiorum ducem" (Freiburg im Breisgau, 1923), p. 16.

[6] Cf. *Codex Juris Canonici,* can. 589 and can. 1366.

[7] Likewise in the Thomas encyclical "Studiorum ducem," p. 18. On the position of St. Thomas within Christian philosophy cf. Fidel G. Martinez, "The Place of St. Thomas in Catholic Philosophy," *Cross Currents,* vol. 8 (New York, 1958), pp. 43 ff.

[8] Albert Mitterer, *Die Entwicklungslehre Augustins im Vergleich mit dem Weltbild des hl. Thomas von Aquin und dem der Gegenwart* (Vienna-Freiberg im Breisgau, 1956), p. 15. Similarly, on p. 327 is the statement: "The Church has . . . prescribed Thomism."

[9] Cf. Étienne Gilson, *The Christian Philosophy of St. Thomas Aquinas* (London, 1957), p. 174; van Steenberghen, *Le XIIIe siècle,* p. 261.

[10] *Christian Philosophy,* p. 174.

[11] Anselm Stolz, "Das Elend der Thomasinterpretation." *Bene-*

diktinische Monatsschrift, Jahrgang 13 (1931). In the same annual volume of this magazine: Stephen Schmutz, "Nach der Lehre des hl. Thomas" (on interpretations of Thomas).

[12] *Shaw on Music.* Ed. by Eric Bentley (New York, 1955), pp. 74 f.

[13] Cf. Josef Pieper, "The Timeliness of Thomism," in *The Silence of St. Thomas* (New York: Pantheon, 1957).

[14] André Hayen, *Thomas gestern und heute* (Frankfurt, 1954), p. 62.

[15] L. B. Geiger, *La Participation dans la philosophie de St. Thomas d'Aquin* (Paris, 1942), p. 31.

[16] Chenu, *Introduction,* pp. 38 ff.

[17] H. C. Scheeben, *Der heilige Dominikus* (Freiburg im Breisgau, 1937), p. 53.

[18] Quoted from Joseph Bernhart, *Sinn der Geschichte* (Freiburg im Breisgau, 1931), p. 53.

[19] Cf. Schnürer, *Kirche und Kultur im Mittelalter,* II, p. 442.

[20] Scheeben, *Dominikus,* p. 229.

[21] Joseph Bernhart, *Der Vatikan als Weltmacht* (Leipzig, 1930), p. 177.

[22] Scheeben, *Dominikus,* p. 43.

[23] Ibid., p. 57.

[24] Ibid., p. 143.

[25] Ibid., p. 135.

[26] Ibid., p. 377.

[27] Ibid., p. 164.

[28] Cf. Franz Xaver Seppelt, *Der Kampf der Bettelorden an der Universität Paris in der Mitte des 13. Jahrhunderts* (two parts), in *Kirchengeschichtliche Abhandlungen,* vol. 3 (Breslau, 1905) and vol. 6 (Breslau, 1908).

[29] Scheeben, *Dominikus,* p. 279.

[30] Cf. Schnürer, *Kirche und Kultur im Mittelalter,* II, p. 365.

[31] C. G. 1, 2.

[32] For example: Contra impugn. 2, 5; Nos. 203, 204, 205, 206.

[33] Contra impugn. 2, 4; No. 205.

[34] I, 65–74 (account of Creation) ; I, II, 98–105 (books of the Law in the Old Testament) ; III, 27–59 (life of Jesus).

[35] Contra impugn. 3; No. 121.

III

[1] *Processus inquisitionis,* cap. 7, 66. *Acta Sanctorum Martii* (Venice, 1735), tom. I, pp. 707 f.

[2] Cf. Schnürer, *Kirche und Kultur im Mittelalter,* II, p. 434.

[3] Ibid.

[4] II, II, 11, 3.

[5] Ibid.

[6] *De secreto* 3.

[7] Ibid.

[8] *Mittelalterliches Geistesleben,* II, p. 67.

[9] Cf. Gilson, *History,* p. 244.

[10] *Mittelalterliches Geistesleben,* II, p. 71.

[11] Ibid.

[12] Ibid., I, p. 259. Cf. also Clemens Baeumker, *Petrus von Hibernia, der Jugendlehrer des Thomas von Aquino,* Sitzungsberichte der Bayer. Akademie der Wissenschaften (Philosoph. Klasse), Munich, 1920.

[13] Grabmann, *Mittelalterliches Geistesleben,* I, p. 261.

IV

[1] The reference is to the textbook by Joseph Gredt, the first Latin edition of which was published in 1899–1901, the German edition in 1935 (both at Freiburg im Breisgau).

[2] Hans Meyer, *Thomas von Aquin* (Bonn, 1938), p. 32.

[3] Marie-Dominique Chenu, "L'équilibre de la scolastique médiévale." *Revue des sciences philosophiques et théologiques,* vol. 29 (1940), p. 312.

[4] In Met. 3, 11; No. 471.

[5] In An. 1, 8; No. 107. Similarly In De Caelo et mundo, 1, 22; 3, 6.

[6] Étienne Gilson, "Le christianisme et la tradition philoso-phique." *Revue des sciences philosophiques et théolo-giques,* vol. 30 (1941–42), p. 254.

[7] Ibid.

[8] Ibid., pp. 249 ff.

[9] ". . . *A sensibilibus recedere nolens* . . ." Substant. separ. 3; No. 18. ". . . *quae sunt manifesta secundum sensum* . . ." Ibid., 2; No. 11. *"Proprium eius philosophiae fuit, a man-ifestis non discedere."* Spir. creat. 5

[10] Letter to Schiller of April 28, 1797.

[11] *Idea of a University* (London, 1921), V, 5, pp. 109 f.

[12] Wilhelm von Hertz, *Gesammelte Aufsätze.* Ed. by Fr. von der Leyen (Stuttgart, 1905), p. 161.

[13] Grabmann, *Mittelalterliches Geistesleben,* II, p. 68.

[14] Ibid., II, 84.

[15] Hans Naumann, *Der staufische Ritter* (Leipzig, 1936), p. 56.

[16] Ibid., p. 92.

[17] Chenu, *Introduction,* p. 29.

[18] Quoted in ibid.

[19] C. G. 2, 4 (1).

[20] Étienne Gilson, *La philosophie au moyen-âge* (Paris, 1947), p. 343.

[21] C. G. 2, 4 (1).

[22] C. G. 2, 3; similarly, C. G. 2, 2 at the end.

[23] Cf. Chenu, *Introduction,* p. 36.

[24] Ibid., p. 6.

[25] Ibid., pp. 108, 113.

[26] In Phys. 8, 2.

[27] I, 1, 8 ad 2.

[28] Quol. 3, 31 ad 1.

[29] I, 1, 8 ad 2.

[30] Cf. on this Josef Pieper, *Uber den Begriff der Tradition* (Cologne–Opladen, 1958), pp. 24 ff.

[31] In Trin. 2, 3 ad 8.

[32] Chenu, *Introduction,* p. 177.

[33] In De caelo et mundo 1, 22.

[34] Ibid.

[35] *In Hexaëmeron* I, 3, 1, 5 (Quarracchi, 1934), p. 92.

[36] Resp. ad Mag. John, 42.

[37] *De anima intellectiva,* cap. 6.

[38] Étienne Gilson, *Der Geist der mittelalterlichen Philosophie* (Vienna, 1950), p. 460.

V

[1] Quol. 4, 18.

[2] Spir. creat. 10, obj. 8, ad 8.

[3] Thus Pico della Mirandola; cf. Grabmann, *Mittelalterliches Geistesleben,* II, p. 85. Similarly, Erasmus of Rotterdam (quoted in Chenu, *Introduction,* p. 43).

[4] Gilson, *Geist der mittelalterlichen Philosophie,* p. 459.

[5] Cf. I. T. Eschmann, "A catalogue of St. Thomas's works," in Gilson, *Christian Philosophy,* p. 407.

[6] In De caelo et mundo 2, 17; No. 451.

[7] In the Latin translation of Aristotle's *Metaphysics* available to Thomas, for example, there is a phrase: *hoc manifestum est* —where the Greek text on the contrary says that it is *not* evident ἄδηλόν ἐστιν; *Metaphysics* 7, 3; 1029a). Nevertheless, Thomas interprets this as if the Latin text also read: hoc *non* manifestum est (In Met. 7, 2; No. 1280.) Other examples of this sort in Chenu, *Introduction,* p. 187, Note 3.

[8] I, 1, 6 ad 3; II, II, 45, 2.

[9] Chenu, *Introduction,* p. 18.

[10] At the beginning of his elucidations of Aristotle's *Physics. Opera Omnia.* Ed. A. Borgnet (Paris, 1890), tom. 3, 1 f.

[11] Cf. Seppelt, *Kampf der Bettelorden,* I, p. 208.

[12] Chenu, *Introduction,* pp. 18 f.

[13] Ibid., p. 17.

[14] Ibid., p. 15.

[15] Ibid., p. 16.

[16] Scheeben, *Dominikus,* p. 151.

[17] Van Steenberghen, *Le XIIIᵉ siècle*, p. 325.

[18] *Die Entstehung der Universitäten des Mittelalters* (Berlin, 1885), p. 46.

[19] On this point I cannot agree with Herbert Grundmann (*Vom Ursprung der Universität im Mittelalter*. Berichte über die Verhandlungen der Sächsischen Akademie der Wissenschaften zu Leipzig. Philosophisch-historische Klasse. Vol. 103, Heft 2 [Berlin, 1957], pp. 62 f.).

VI

[1] Chenu, *Introduction*, p. 22.

[2] More detail in Seppelt, *Kampf der Bettelorden*, and in Max Bierbaum, *Bettelorden und Weltgeistlichkeit an der Universität Paris* (Münster, 1920).

[3] Cf. Seppelt, *Kampf der Bettelorden*, Introduction.

[4] Contra impugn., No. 407.

[5] Ibid., No. 418.

[6] *Determinationes quaestionum* 1, 27 (*Opera omnia* 8, 355); quoted in Bierbaum, *Bettelorden*, p. 244.

[7] Seppelt, *Kampf der Bettelorden*, II, p. 82.

[8] Scheeben, *Dominikus*, p. 269.

[9] Ibid., p. 288.

[10] Seppelt, *Kampf der Bettelorden*, I, p. 209.

[11] Bierbaum, *Bettelorden*, p. 245.

[12] Seppelt, *Kampf der Bettelorden*, I, p. 209.

[13] Van Steenberghen, *Le XIIIᵉ siècle*, pp. 289, 291.

[14] Seppelt, *Kampf der Bettelorden*, I, p. 216.

[15] Ibid., II, pp. 88 ff.

[16] The complete Latin text is to be found in Bierbaum, *Bettelorden*.

[17] Herbert Grundmann, *Religiöse Bewegungen im Mittelalter* (Berlin, 1935), p. 156.

[18] Quol. 5, 26.

[19] Contra retrah. 14, No. 833 (5).

[20] Ibid., 16; No. 854.

VII

[1] Contra retrah. 16; No. 856.

[2] Ibid., final sentences.

[3] Un. int., at end.

[4] Contra impugn., No. 260 (2).

[5] Ibid., No. 260 (3).

[6] Ibid., No. 260 (6).

[7] Ibid., No. 260 (11).

[8] This has been done, for example, in Carl Prantl's *Geschichte der Logik im Abendlande,* still considered a standard text. More detail on this matter in Josef Pieper, *Wahrheit der Dinge* (3rd ed.; Munich, 1957), pp. 35 f; pp. 122 f.

[9] Seventh letter, 341 c.

[10] *Sophistes* 263 e.

[11] *Metaphysics* 3, 1; 995 a.

[12] *Topics* 8, 11; 161 a.

[13] Martin Grabmann, *Die Geschichte der scholastischen Methode* (Freiburg im Breisgau 1909–11), II, p. 18.

[14] *Metalogicus* 3, 10.

[15] Quoted in Grabmann, *Scholastische Methode,* II, p. 20.

[16] Ibid., II, pp. 120 ff.

[17] *Philosophie der Weltgeschichte* (Leipzig, 1923), IV, p. 859.

[18] Plato, *Gorgias* 449.

[19] *Thomas von Aquin,* p. 41; *Einführung in die Summa theologiae des hl. Thomas von Aquin* (Freiburg im Breisgau, 1919), pp. 53 ff.

[20] I, II, 24, 3.

[21] Cf. also Ver. 26, 7 ad 1.

[22] Gilson, *History,* p. 325.

[23] Chenu, *Introduction,* p. 241.

[24] Ibid., p. 245. Pierre Mandonnet, "St. Thomas, créateur de la dispute quodlibétique," *Revue des sciences philosophiques et théologiques,* vols. 15–16 (1926–27).

[25] Chenu, *Introduction,* p. 291.

[26] Plato, *Phaedo* 91; 95.

[27] Quoted in Chenu, *Introduction,* p. 164.

[28] C. G. 1, 2.

[29] In Met. 12, 9; No. 2566.

[30] Augustine, *Contra epistolam Manichaei quam vocant fundamenti*, 2.

[31] John Henry Cardinal Newman, *An Essay in Aid of a Grammar of Assent* (5th ed.; London: Burns & Oates, 1881), p. 162.

[32] William of Tocco, *Vita*, 5, 27. On St. Thomas' polemical style cf. P. Glorieux, "Un maître polémiste: Thomas d'Aquin," *Mélanges de science religieuse*, vol. 5 (Lille, 1948).

[33] C. G. 3, 48.

[34] Per. vit. spir. 26; No. 734.

[35] *Blätter und Steine* (Hamburg, 1934), p. 226.

[36] Preface to the second edition of 1787 (edition of the Philosophische Bibliothek, ed. by R. Schmidt [Leipzig, 1930], p. 36).

[37] Grabmann, *Scholastische Methode*, II, pp. 349 ff.

VIII

[1] Chenu, *Introduction*, p. 175.

[2] Contra err. Graec., proemium; No. 1030.

[3] Cf. Franz Xaver Seppelt, *Geschichte der Päpste* (2nd ed.; Munich, 1954 ff.), III, pp. 523 ff.

[4] III, 79, 5. Cf. also Josef Pieper, "Randbemerkungen zum Herrenmahl-Traktat der Summa theologica," in *Weistum, Dichtung, Sakrament* (Munich, 1954), pp. 286 ff.

[5] C. G. 1, 2.

[6] William of Tocco, *Vita*, 8, 48.

[7] Cf. Josef Pieper, "Thomas von Aquin als Lehrer," in *Weistum, Dichtung, Sakrament*. A section of the following pages is taken verbatim from this treatise.

[8] Grabmann has arranged his already cited *Einführung in die Summa theologiae* as an elucidation of this preface.

[9] William of Tocco, *Vita*, 3, 15.

[10] Erich Przywara entitled a highly interesting essay (*Stimmen der Zeit,* Jahrgang 1925): "Thomas als Problematiker." In his subsequently published collection of essays, *Ringen der Gegenwart,* this apparently somewhat offensive title was changed to a more neutral one: "Thomas von Aquin."

[11] Chenu, *Introduction,* p. 81.

[12] Quol. 6, 19.

[13] Quol. 3, 27.

[14] Quol. 8, 13; 9, 15.

[15] Quol. 11, 12.

[16] Quol. 12, 20.

[17] Chenu, *Introduction,* p. 254.

[18] C. G. 1, 2.

[19] Cf. Chenu, *Introduction,* p. 273.

[20] 1 d. 14, 2, 2; cf. also 1 d. 2, divisio textus.

IX

[1] Chenu, *Introduction,* p. 88.

[2] Hegel, *Vorlesungen über die Geschichte der Philosophie.* Jubiläumsausgabe, ed. by H. Glockner (Stuttgart, 1928), vol. 19, p. 99.

[3] Ludwig Traube, *Einleitung in die lateinische Philologie des Mittelalters* (Munich, 1911), p. 44.

[4] Karl Vossler, *Geist und Kultur in der Sprache* (Heidelberg, 1925), p. 57.

[5] P. Lehmann, *Erforschung des Mittelalters* (Leipzig, 1941), p. 64.

[6] Ludwig Bieler, "Das Mittellatein als Sprachproblem." *Lexis* (Heidegger *Festschrift*), vol. 2, p. 104.

[7] Ibid.

[8] Richard Meister, "Mittellatein als Traditionssprache." In *Liber Floridus* (P. Lehmann *Festschrift*), (St. Ottilien, 1950).

[9] Christine Mohrmann, "Le dualisme de la Latinité médiévale."

Revue des Études Latines, vol. 29 (Paris, 1951). Cf. also M. Hubert, "Quelques aspects du Latin philosophique aux XIIe et XIIIe siècles," *Revue des Études Latines,* vol. 27 (Paris, 1949).

[10] Ibid., pp. 338–41.

[11] Ibid., p. 338.

[12] Ibid., p. 339.

[13] Ibid., p. 348.

[14] Chenu, *Introduction,* p. 90.

[15] Ibid., p. 97.

[16] Quoted ibid., p. 98.

[17] Seneca, *Letters to Lucilius,* 117, 5.

[18] Chenu, *Introduction,* p. 97.

[19] Augustine, *Confessions,* 10, 27. (*The Confessions of St. Augustine.* Translated by Edward B. Pusey, D.D. [New York: Pocket Books, Inc., 1951], pp. 195–96.)

[20] C. G. 2, 3.

[21] III, 64, 5 ad 2.

[22] F. A. Blanche, "Sur la langue technique de Saint Thomas d'Aquin." *Revue de Philosophie,* vol. 30 (Paris, 1930).

[23] Ibid., p. 13 f.

[24] Ibid., p. 15 f.

[25] Ibid., p. 16 f.

[26] Ibid., p. 15.

[27] Alfons Hufnagel, *Studien zur Entwicklung des thomistischen Erkenntnisbegriffes im Anschluss an das Correctorium "Quare"* (Münster, 1935), p. 105.

[28] Chenu, *Introduction,* p. 102.

[29] *Topics,* 2, 2; 110a; quoted by Thomas, for example, in the first chapter of the *Summa Against the Pagans.*

[30] Blanche, "Langue technique," p. 25.

[31] Ver. 4, 2.

[32] I, 4, 3 ad 4; 1 d. 28, 2, 2.

[33] Goethe in a letter to Schiller dated July 9, 1796.

[34] *In Hexaëmeron* 22, 21 (*Opera Omnia,* 5, 440).

[35] Virt. card. 1 ad 10.

[36] Cf. Alois Dempf. *Sacrum Imperium* (Munich, 1929), p. 303.
[37] Contra impugn., No. 531.
[38] 13, 2.

X

[1] In John, 1, 5.
[2] Pot. 5, 10 ad 5.
[3] II, II, 142, 1; 152, 2 ad 2; 153, 3 ad 3.
[4] I, II, 23, 1 ad 1; 23, 3; I, 81, 2.
[5] II, II, 23, 1 ad 1; 23, 3; I, 81, 2.
[6] I, 98, 2.
[7] New York: Pantheon, 1950.
[8] Ibid., p. 178.
[9] Ibid., p. 179.
[10] "If thy eye is single (*simplex*), the whole of thy body will
    be lit up." Matthew 6, 22.
[11] C. G. 4, 58; similarly, III, 65.
[12] Cf. B. Altaner, *Patrologie* (Freiburg im Breisgau, 1955), p.
    419.
[13] Van Steenberghen, *Le XIIIe siècle*, p. 275.
[14] Ibid., pp. 266, 272.
[15] Van Steenberghen has shown (ibid., pp. 278 ff.), with sound
    arguments, that this statement is inapplicable. The philos-
    ophy of Siger of Brabant, he says, might just as well be
    called Plotinic as Avicennistic or Thomistic or Averroistic.
    "Latin Averroism," he points out, existed only in the
    imagination of Ernest Renan (p. 280).
[16] Gilson, *History*, p. 408.
[17] Ibid., p. 407.
[18] A. G. Little, *The Platonic Heritage of Thomism* (Dublin,
    1949), p. 12.
[19] Cf. Gilson, *History*, p. 382.
[20] C. G. 3, 69.
[21] G. M. Manser, *Das Wesen des Thomismus* (3rd ed.; Frei-
    burg, Switzerland, 1949), p. 213.

[22] In John 1, 17.
[23] C. G. 4, 56.

XI

[1] Cf. Josef Pieper, "Was heisst 'christliches Abendland'?" In *Überlieferung und Neubeginn* (Ratingen, 1957). Also: Pieper, "Die Frage nach dem christlichen Abendland," in *Europa: Vermächtnis und Verpflichtung,* ed. by Hansgeorg Loebel (Frankfurt, 1957).

[2] *Christian Philosophy,* p. 83.

[3] In Met. 9, 5; No. 1826.

[4] C. G., 1, 22.

[5] Gilson, *History,* p. 365.

[6] Aristotle, *Metaphysics,* 1948 a.

[7] Étienne Gilson, "Maimonide et la philosophie de l'Exode." *Mediaeval Studies,* vol. 13 (Toronto, 1951).

[8] Jacques Maritain, "L'humanisme de St. Thomas d'Aquin." *Mediaeval Studies,* vol. 3 (Toronto, 1941).

[9] Gilson, *Christian Philosophy,* p. 368. Cf. also on this subject Benoît Pruche, "Le thomisme, peut-il se présenter comme 'philosophie existentielle'?" *Revue philosophique de Louvain,* tom. 48 (1950).

[10] Gilson, *Christian Philosophy,* pp. 48 ff.

[11] Augustine, *Tractatus in Joannis Evangelium,* 28, 8, 8–10; Migne, *Patrologia Latina* 35, 1678 f.

[12] *De trinitate* 7, 5, 10; Migne, *Patrologia Latina,* 42, 942.

[13] Gilson, *Christian Philosophy,* p. 93.

[14] I, 8, 1.

[15] Gilson, *Christian Philosophy,* p. 139.

[16] *"Essentia dicitur secundum quod per eam et in ea ens habet esse." De ente et essentia,* cap. 1, 3.

[17] Comp. theol. 1, 68; No. 119.

[18] I, 8, 1.

[19] Ibid.

[20] C. G. 2, 22.

[21] Gilson, *Christian Philosophy*, p. 374

[22] In Hebd. 3; No. 50.

[23] Gilson, *Christian Philosophy*, p. 374.

[24] Ibid., p. 8.

[25] Cf. J. de Guibert, *Les doublets de St. Thomas d'Aquin. Leur étude méthodique* (Paris, 1926).

[26] 1 Sent., prolog. 1, 1 ad 1; 2 Sent., prolog.

[27] C. G., 2, 4.

[28] I, 1, 1 ad 2.

[29] I, 1, 1 ad 2.

[30] I, 1, 3.

[31] *Philebus* 16 c.

[32] *Gorgias* 523 a; 527 a.

[33] II, II, 2, 7 ad 3; 3 d. 25, 2, 2, 2 ad 3; Ver. 14, 11 ad 5.

[34] Cf. on this, Pieper, *Über den Begriff der Tradition*, pp. 29 ff.

XII

[1] "*Philosophi . . . creatures considerant, secundum quod in propria natura consistunt.*" 2 Sent. prolog.—"*Philosophia determinat de existentibus secundum rationes a creaturis sumptas.*" 1 Sent. prolog., 1 ad 1.—"*. . . creaturas secundum se considerat.*" C. G. 2, 4.

[2] C. G. 1, 4.

[3] *Timaeus* 29–30.

[4] *Nomoi* 715 e.

[5] *Philebus* 30 d.

[6] *Phaedo* 63 c.

[7] *Menon* 81 f.

[8] C. G. 2, 4.

[9] Ver. 14, 9 ad 8.

[10] Contra impugn. 3, 5; No. 411.

[11] C. G. 2, 3.

[12] *Briefwechsel mit dem Grafen Yorck von Wartenburg* (Halle, 1923), p. 39.

[13] Gilson, *Christian Philosophy*, p. 94.

[14] Ibid., p. 443.

[15] Martin Grabmann, *Theologische Erkenntnis—und Einlei-tungslehre des heiligen Thomas von Aquin* (Freiburg, Switzerland, 1948), p. 183.

[16] *Metaphysics* 1, 2; 982 a 18.

[17] In Met. 1, 2; No. 42.

[18] I, 1, 5, sed contra.

[19] Cf. Grabmann, *Theologische Erkenntnislehre*, p. 183.

[20] Cf. C. G. 2, 4.

[21] Contra impugn. 3, 4; No. 400.

[22] Ibid., 3, 4; No. 399.

[23] Cf. Vatican Council, *Constitutio de fide catholica,* cap. 4 (Denzinger No. 1796). Also: M. J. Scheeben, *Die Mys-terien des Christentums,* ed. by J. Höfer (Freiburg in Breisgau, 1941), pp. 8 f.

[24] Oxford University Sermons 4 (June 1, 1841).

[25] Friedrich von Huegel, *Andacht zur Wirklichkeit.* Schriften in Auswahl; ed. by M. Schlüter-Hermkes (Munich, 1952), pp. 223, 225.

[26] "*. . . Utitur.*" 1 Sent., prolog. 1, 1.— "*. . . supponit.*" In Trin. 2, 3.

[27] *Phänomenologie des Geistes,* Vorrede. Ed. by J. Hoffmeister (Hamburg, 1952), p. 12.

[28] Chenu, *Introduction,* p. 158.

[29] Aymé Forest in his review of Geiger's book, *La participation dans la philosophie de St. Thomas d'Aquin. Revue des sciences philosophiques et théologiques,* vol. 30 (1941–42), p. 471.

[30] I, 3, prolog.

[31] Pot. 7, 5 ad 14.

[32] In Hebd. 2; No. 23.

[33] Ver. 10, 1.

[34] Cf. Josef Pieper, "The Negative Element in the Philosophy of St. Thomas Aquinas," in *The Silence of St. Thomas* (New York: Pantheon, 1957).

INDEX

179